D1175598

ACCOUNTING PUBLICATIONS
OF
SCHOLARS BOOK CO.

Editor, Robert R. Sterling

Accounting Classics Series

Publication of this Classic was made possible
by a grant from Price Waterhouse Foundation

Suggestions of titles to be included
in the Series are solicited and should
be addressed to the Editor.

CHANGING CONCEPTS
OF Business Income

CHANGING CONCEPTS OF BUSINESS INCOME

REPORT OF STUDY GROUP ON BUSINESS INCOME

Scholars Book Co.
4431 Mt. Vernon
Houston, Texas 77006

Library of Congress Card Catalog Number: 75-21163
ISBN: 0-914348-18-3
Manufactured in the United States of America

Foreword

The scope and purpose of this report are indicated in the letter of the Secretary of the American Institute of Accountants to The Rockefeller Foundation included in Exhibit I.

The movements and controversies of these times involve accounting in constantly increasing measure. Resort to it is made to support many causes, whose conflicting interests become the origin of divergent views on accounting questions.

Those responsible for this report present it in the hope of making this situation better known and understood, and of moving towards a larger agreement among the differing lines of thought now prevalent. That these differences are still large is clear from the report, but it is believed that they have been reduced by the discussions of the group, and that agreement may grow further as the report becomes better known. The wide variety of viewpoint will be clear from the names and affiliations of the members of the group.

After several years of discussion and the circulation of material among the members of the Study Group, the original drafting of this report was entrusted to George O. May who associated with him Oswald W. Knauth. Individual sections were written by Arthur Dean and Solomon Fabricant. After consideration by the Study Group a sub-committee of May, Werntz and Greer was appointed to revise the report. The extent to which they have labored to make it reflect the views of the entire group is apparent on every page; their efforts towards reconciliation have been unremitting. The dissents and comments round out the discussion in the text itself.

Members of the Study Group were asked to ballot on approving the report for publication, and the large majority have so voted. As stated in the report, it is not to be assumed that every member so voting approves of every detail of the report. Members of the group have in many cases waived their individual preferences on matters of minor importance in order to achieve a report on which there could be substantial agreement.

Probably all members feel that the study has achieved its greatest contribution in bringing so many diverse minds to bear on the problem, in reaching as much agreement as has been achieved, and in offering a comprehensive basis for further study.

PERCIVAL F. BRUNDAGE
Chairman of Study Group on Business Income

CONTENTS

SECTION 1

Introduction

1. The growth in importance of income determinations in the social and economic life of the nation is a marked characteristic of the last half-century. During the same period the increase in size and complexity of business enterprises has made the determination of business income more difficult, and more essentially an accounting task.

2. The American Institute of Accountants has long been conscious of the responsibilities of the profession that arise from these conditions. Its contribution toward a better understanding of the problems involved first took the form of committees on cooperation with bodies such as those of credit men, banks, and stock exchanges, and later with the Securities and Exchange Commission.

3. As its resources increased, the Institute undertook, in 1938, the creation of a broader organization—a Committee on Accounting Procedure to which was attached a Research Department.

4. Early in the last decade the Institute contemplated plans for bringing about a study of the more fundamental problems by a body representative not only of accountancy but of other disciplines. The war delayed its efforts to carry out this plan, but in 1947 it secured cooperation and a matching grant from The Rockefeller Foundation for the creation of a Study Group whose function would be to consider the concepts and terminology of business income.

5. This Group, which was organized along lines similar to those adopted by the National Bureau of Economic Research, has consisted of some forty or fifty members with an Executive Committee of six, composed in equal numbers of accountants and nonaccountants.*

* In Exhibit I there will be found (1) a copy of the letter addressed to The Rockefeller Foundation setting forth the objectives; (2) a list of those who have participated in the work of the Group; (3) a list of members of the Executive Committee.

6. The Group decided to approach the subject from the standpoints of accounting, law, and economics.

7. In Section 2 of the following, the Group considers the general concepts of income. Since concepts must be implemented by accounting, the Group has deemed it appropriate next to furnish in Section 3, as background, a brief historical account of the development of present accounting principles or conventions. In order to place the problem in proper perspective, there is presented in Sections 4 and 5 a discussion of important accounting developments in recent years which serve to illustrate the kinds of practical questions that arise. Sections 6 and 7 deal with concepts of business income from the economic and legal viewpoints. The report ends with a summary and statement of the conclusions to which the study has led.

8. At all points opportunities have been offered for the presentation of dissenting views. For convenience these have been brought together in Section 9.

9. Throughout the study it has been necessary to consider not only what might be wished for, but also what could in practice be attained. Income determination has been, and will remain, a compromise between theory and practicability.

10. In the double-entry system accounting has long possessed a rigorous and universal method of analysis. But the objectives of the analysis and the assumptions on which it shall be based have always to be settled in advance.

11. The assumptions appropriate for a determination of business income cannot be deduced from, or verified by, the study of natural laws. Just as in law "fictions" are adopted, so accounting for business income must adopt conventions, postulates, or principles, the choice of which initially must be governed by a variety of considerations. Among these are the use to be made of the determination of business income and practicability and regard for the fiscal, legal, and economic conditions under which the enterprise is to operate.

12. Conclusions reached by accounting do not therefore possess the inevitability that is suggested by the method of analysis employed. Nor can they have the precision or factual character which the form of presentation often leads the reader to attribute to them. Their useful-

ness rests in part on the validity of the postulates adopted, in part on the appropriateness of the methods employed for implementing those postulates, in part on the skill and objectivity with which those methods of implementation have been applied, and in part on the clarity and fullness with which the results are presented.

13. The American Institute of Accountants in suggesting the present study was fully cognizant of these facts. In a quotation from its first *Accounting Research Bulletin,* which accompanied the letter to The Rockefeller Foundation requesting support for this study, its Committee had said, in 1939:

> The committee regards corporation accounting as one phase of the working of the corporate organization of business, which in turn it views as a machinery created by the people in the belief that, broadly speaking, it will serve a useful social purpose. The test of the corporate system and of the special phase of it represented by corporate accounting ultimately lies in the results which are produced. These results must be judged from the standpoint of society as a whole—not from that of any one group of interested parties.
>
> The uses to which the corporate system is put and the controls to which it is subject change from time to time, and all parts of the machinery must be adapted to meet such changes as they occur.

14. The relation of changes in price levels to the determination of income is manifestly of crucial importance. In Exhibit II is presented a chart, made available by courtesy of Dun & Bradstreet, Inc., showing the changes in price levels and in purchasing power during the century ending in 1950. The changes in prices that have taken place in the last twenty-five years have emphasized the importance of this phase of the general problem which the Group undertook to study, and the present report is, therefore, largely devoted to it.

The fact that the last quarter of the nineteenth century (in which accounting began to assume wider importance) was one in which the trend of prices was downward, while in the present century the trend has been upward, is significant.

15. As will be seen from the Summary and Conclusions, the Group recommends as a goal an expansion of the framework of accounting statements designed to distinguish between the results of activities

measured in units of substantially equal purchasing power and the effects of changes in the purchasing power of the monetary unit. Pending the attainment of this goal, the Group believes that supplementary information that will facilitate such an analysis might helpfully be furnished in annual reports of those corporations whose securities are widely distributed, and recommends that as far as possible this information should be part of the material upon which the independent accountant expresses his opinion.

16. The Group believes that the recommendations and the conclusions set forth in Section 8 find ample support in the evidence presented in Sections 2 to 7 of the report.

17. The fact that a member of the Group has signed the report does not imply his acceptance of responsibility for statements made in the technical sections, but only that, except to the extent of an express dissent, he concurs in the Summary and Conclusions contained in Section 8.

SECTION 2

Concepts of Income

1. Income is the name given to a family of concepts in the world of ideas closely related to those of wealth and value. The family includes a number of branches, some of which are commonly referred to by compound names, such as personal income, business income, gross income, net income, taxable income (though once the limitation has been indicated the narrowing adjective is, unfortunately, often ignored in later discussion), national income, etc. The name enjoys great prestige, which has been enhanced by its use in constitutional or legislative enactments, among the most important of these being the Sixteenth Amendment to our Constitution, and the extensive use of income taxation. The name is used freely in law, finance, business, economics, and accounting, either with or without modification.

2. In general the courts have been cautious about defining income, as they have been about defining fraud, because definition involves exclusion and aids the would-be evader of the law. They have interpreted it differently in different contexts. In the monograph which he prepared for the Study Group, Arthur H. Dean mentioned nearly a dozen uses for which income determinations become necessary.

3. Our Supreme Court, when called upon to interpret the word as used in the Sixteenth Amendment, defined income as the gain derived from capital, from labor, or from both combined. Significantly, the Court did not deem it necessary to state explicitly that gain might be measured by comparing money received with money paid without regard to changes in the real value of the monetary unit. Its definition may appear merely to substitute the problem of defining "gain" for that of defining "income," but it is valuable in that it suggests three main classifications of income: income from personal service, income from investment, and income from business.

5

4. The lines between these classifications are not, of course, clearly drawn; the wage earner may employ a small amount of capital in the form of tools which he owns, and the individual may contribute study and judgment to the earning of investment income. Nevertheless, this broad classification is helpful for the purpose of analysis.

5. Economists use the term in widely varying senses, depending on the purpose for which income is calculated. Indeed, O. C. Stine has suggested that writers should be encouraged to indicate the precise concept they are expounding by classification and subclassification. Other economists have suggested that economic statisticians develop a variety of concepts, some, for example, inclusive of capital gains and losses (realized or unrealized), some exclusive of them. Economists are keenly aware of the difficulties of defining income. J. R. Hicks has said that in dynamic economics (that is, economic analysis which takes account of time intervals) "savings" and "income" are tools that break in our hands.

6. Increases in capital value constitute an important source of accretion to wealth; thus their relationship to the concept of income requires consideration. They may be regarded as outside the category, or as a part of investment income, or as sometimes a part of investment income and sometimes a part of business income. Practical difficulties stand in the way of attributing them in part to personal service, except where investment becomes a business.

7. A review of accounting literature indicates that accountants use the term in materially different senses. There are differences of opinion among them regarding the limits of the responsibilities they can wisely assume and the nature of the judgments they should undertake.

8. The Study Group has limited its consideration to business income, but manifestly it is necessary to consider this classification in relation to broad concepts of income.

The Broad Concept of Income

9. The question, What is income? lacks body unless it is amplified by the indication of a period and a recipient or beneficiary so that it takes the form, What is income in a given period to a given person or entity? But the allocation of any but the simplest forms of income to a period

such as a year can only be conventional. Naturally, the form of the convention will be determined largely by the object, or objects, for which income determinations are desired, and by the mode of thought of the time or of those by whom it is formulated.

10. Irving Fisher has written:

Like many other concepts of general familiarity and fundamental importance in economics, income is still a controversial subject; and the fact that income must be defined for taxation purposes . . . does not help matters.[1]

11. A few quotations will suffice to illustrate a variety of historical points of view.

. . . the mercantilist's notion of income resembled the balance of profit on the merchant's books at the close of the year . . . the physiocrats boldly identified it with the *produit net* of the progressive agricultural entrepreneur.[2]

12. Adam Smith's classic definition of gross revenue (1776) is:

The whole annual produce of . . . land and labor [and of] net revenue [is] what remains free . . . after deducting the expense of maintaining first . . . fixed and secondly circulating capital.

Net income to individuals, in his view, is

what without encroaching upon their capital they can place in their stock reserves for immediate consumption.

13. Many definitions emphasize the recurring character of income. In Germany, however, G. Schanz (1896) regarded as income

the entire difference between the value of assets at the end of the fiscal period and their value at the beginning, thus including every accretion— in money or kind, regular or irregular, from continuous or temporary sources—deducting only interest payments and capital losses.

In this view he was followed by R. M. Haig, who stated in 1920:

Income is the money value of the net accretion to economic power between two points in time.

[1] Quoted from Irving Fisher's article on "Income" in *Encyclopaedia of the Social Sciences*, VII, pp. 623–625.
[2] *Ibid.*, p. 625.

14. Irving Fisher's own definition of income (1932) was as follows:

> The income of society as a whole is the total money value of all the services received by the members of society from all sources. . . . Most events are interactions; so that in a comprehensive view most services are also disservices and cancel out, leaving as a final uncanceled fringe only the psychic experiences—enjoyable or distasteful—of the consumer.[3]

15. While his concept defined income as what is received, he contemplated that it should be measured by what is spent. He admitted, in what was perhaps an understatement, that his definition could not be said as yet to represent the common opinion of all, or even most, students.

16. More recently, J. R. Hicks has said in his *Value and Capital,* first published in England in 1939:

> The purpose of income calculations in practical affairs is to give people an indication of the amount which they can consume without impoverishing themselves. Following out this idea, it would seem that we ought to define a man's income as the maximum value which he can consume during a week, and still expect to be as well off at the end of the week as he was at the beginning.[4]

But he concluded that this concept of income was not a useful tool for dynamic economic analysis.

17. The Haig definition raises the question, What is meant by economic power? He and others have suggested that it should be measured in terms of *immediate* command over *goods and services*. Others, such as C. C. Plehn, have taken the position that the command must be regarded as exercisable over time.

18. In the concept quoted from J. R. Hicks, the question becomes, What is meant by "as well off"? Should the comparison be made in terms of a command over goods and services or of money?

19. Sidney S. Alexander, in the monograph which he prepared for the Study Group, adopted the concept of J. R. Hicks and interpreted it as calling for periodical determination of the present value of all future expectations, and income as including a regular flow and a

[3] *Ibid.,* p. 623.
[4] 2nd ed. (The Clarendon Press, 1946), p. 172.

change in the capital value of such a flow or of any other expectation, and also casual or nonrecurring profits.

20. He stated that the "capitalization" concept was not applicable to the expectations of the individual of yield from his own efforts. This raises the questions of what is meant by expectation and whether the concept is properly applicable to expectations which, from a practical point of view, stand on much the same footing as those growing out of personal service.

21. Dealing with the latter point, we may, for instance, compare the position of A receiving a salary under a contract which calls for an increase ultimately to a much higher level, and carries a right to a future pension, with that of B, who has acquired an expectancy of a life interest to begin upon the happening of some future event. It is difficult to see upon what theory the discounting process should be applied to determine present income in the case of B but not in that of A.

22. Again, upon what conceptual ground is the present value of A's expectations to be excluded from his income while the expectations of a shopkeeper (whether carrying on business as an individual or through a corporation) is to be included in his? No satisfactory answer to this question can be based on the ground of greater probability of realization or ease of evaluation; the future of the employee is likely to be better assured and more easily discounted than that of the shopkeeper. Nor can it be based on the ground of magnitude, for compensation is sometimes larger than the profits of a business; nor on the ground of any essential difference in nature.

23. It is not easy to see how the capitalization type of concept could be implemented or be useful in economic analysis in the determination of national income. And a flow of income and a change in the value of expectations would seem to differ in essential characteristics sufficiently to make their treatment in separate categories desirable, even though each may be regarded as an appropriate subject for taxation. The British Inland Revenue Authorities in 1920 took the position that if "capital gains" were to be taxed, the levy should not be made under the income tax law. Neither in the United States nor in England has any proposal to tax *unrealized* gains (capital or other) received serious consideration from the legislature, tax authorities, or the courts.

24. It is not necessary at this point to pursue this line of discussion. It is sufficient to observe that the capitalization concept is not claimed to be acceptable as a *general* concept of income. Only its appropriateness for use in the restricted area of business income will be considered here.

25. If we turn from theory to practice, we find that interest is universally regarded as income without regard to changes either in the monetary or in the real value of the principal on which it is paid. If an individual buys a 2½ per cent Government bond at par of $100 and holds it for a year, he is said to have received income of $2.50 even though the monetary value of the bond and the interest together is no more, or even less, than $100; or though the value of the dollar has diminished. If he sells the bond just after the end of the year for $97.50 he may still, in common usage and in law, be said to have had income of $2.50 for the year. It would seem, therefore, that the concept of income as a flow has as much support in theory as the concept of it as an increase in the capitalized value of future expectations, and that it has more support in practice. Obviously, it is more readily capable of being implemented and less markedly subjective in character.

Influence of Income Taxation, United Kingdom

26. Before the days of the classical economists or income taxation, a right to the yield from property, particularly land, was often vested for a period of years in a person other than the owner of the property or of the reversionary interest therein. For this purpose income was conceived as the *flow* or the *fruit,* capital being regarded as the *source* or the *tree.* The same concept was, of course, applicable to income from labor.

27. The classical economists, beginning with Adam Smith, were interested in national income, or as it is sometimes called, the net national product or national dividend. The concept of a flow was appropriate for this purpose.

28. With the industrial revolution came the mode of thought, reflected in the development of commercial law under Mansfield, that the interpretation of business terms such as income was to be determined by the practices of businessmen.

29. In 1842 income was adopted by the British Government as a major basis of taxation, to which use it had previously been put only in times of war, notably between 1798 and 1815. For two-thirds of a century after 1842, the tax was levied on all income beyond a modest exemption at a uniform and, by modern standards, low rate which varied from less than 1 per cent to nearly 7 per cent. For this purpose also the concept of a flow was suitable.

30. It is sometimes said that the English concept of taxable income which excludes changes in capital value was originally, and is still, dominated by the thinking of an agricultural economy. But there is room for difference of opinion on this.

31. Lawrence H. Seltzer, for instance, in discussing the development in England of the concept of taxable income said in 1945:

> The concept of income that evolved for this purpose was evolved at a time when landed property comprised the bulk of all property, and when a man's estate could therefore be usefully regarded as a physical entity.

He commented:

> The distinction still made by lawyers and the courts between income and a realized "accretion to capital" now sounds archaic to nearly everyone else.

32. His next step was to question the validity of a distinction between realized and unrealized accretions in the taxation of income, as have other writers on the subject of taxable income.

33. There is something fascinating about the idea that for 150 years the United Kingdom, which during the greater part of the time was either the first manufacturing or the first financial power of the world, or both, should base its most important tax on the thinking of an agricultural economy. But the facts do not seem to bear out such theory.

34. Even when the younger Pitt introduced his first income tax proposal in 1798, *The Wealth of Nations* had been in active circulation for more than twenty years. Pitt, like Shelburne before him, was a disciple of Adam Smith; landlord's rentals constituted less than 20 per cent of Pitt's first estimate of taxable income;[5] Mansfield had died in retire-

---

[5] S. Dowell, *History of Taxes and Taxation in England*, 2nd ed. (Longmans Green & Co., 1888), II, p. 224.

ment six years earlier, after completing his great work of placing commercial law on the basis of business custom.

35. The Government of Sir Robert Peel that revived the income tax in 1842 was the Government that repealed the Corn Laws; it represented the new industrial, not the old agricultural, interest. The same Government, it may be noted, enacted the Company Clauses Acts of 1845 which provided for limitation of profits of such enterprises as gas and water companies; under these Acts, and the later Regulation of Railways Act of 1868, income was determined by the double-account system which treated the enterprise as permanent, and which will be of crucial interest when business income comes to be discussed hereinafter.

36. The mode of thought which led to the adoption of rules which have frequently been claimed to reflect an agricultural viewpoint is perhaps rather that indicated by a passage from Paragraph 186 of the famous *Report of the Royal Commission on the Income Tax,* 1920:

> . . . as all material assets waste, and as no income emerges from a source which is so permanent as not to be subject to the possibility of wastage in capital value, there shall be a time limit to the recognition of wastage. In fixing this time, regard should be paid, we think, only to that wastage which is important when considered in relation to human life and human expectation. If a man has an income which will apparently last for 60 years it is to him practically a permanent income. Contingencies happening after the lapse of a period of time exceeding 35 years appeal very little to the mind of the average individual; for example, it is only when the period of deferment is something less than 35 years that reversionary interests begin to have any appreciable value.

On a 6 per cent basis the difference in value between an annuity for 35 years and a perpetuity of the same amount is only 13 per cent; extend the 35 years to 50 and it falls to 5½ per cent.

This approach is similar in its practical effect to the adoption of the postulate of permanence that has an important place in the determination of business income.

37. The English courts have consistently held that what was *business* income was, in the absence of specific provisions of law to the contrary, to be determined by business practice.

Influence of Income Taxation, United States

38. In 1909 a new and vitally important policy of graduated income taxation was inaugurated in England, and as a result of wars and changes in social outlook the graduation has since become steep.

39. In the United States Federal taxation of income of individuals became possible only with the adoption of the Sixteenth Amendment in 1913. We have gone through much the same stages as the English, but in much shorter time.

40. The question whether accretions to capital value may be regarded as income either upon or prior to realization became of major political importance with the adoption of the Sixteenth Amendment, which constitutes the sole authority for Federal taxation of individuals in respect of their ownership of wealth or its fruits. The Supreme Court early decided that realized capital gains might be regarded as income. The question whether unrealized gains might be taxed was considered in the stock-dividend cases. The Court then held that there was no income without "severance."

The validity of this proposition has been questioned. In 1922 T. R. Powell, in a discussion, made the comment, which has often been cited, that, "From a practical common sense point of view there is something strange in the idea that a man may indefinitely grow richer without ever being subject to an income tax." But a tax on becoming richer is not necessarily the same as a tax on income. A stream of recurrent income, a realized increment in the capital value of that stream, an unrealized increase in that capital value, a gift and a legacy, are surely sufficiently different phenomena to be given different names even though all may tend to make an individual richer.

41. In a more recent dividend case, *Helvering* v. *Griffiths,* 318 U.S. 371 (1943), Mr. Justice Douglas quoted Powell and said the severance test would "not stand analysis." But the question at issue in these cases was *when* what was admittedly income (of the recurrent type) realized by a corporation could properly be taxed to the stockholder, an issue which involved also the nature of the corporation. There was some authority for the view that the law might look through the

corporation to the stockholder, and that profits of a corporation might be taxed to the stockholder without distribution having been made. The Court said that "the narrow question here is whether Congress has the power to make the receipt of a stock dividend the occasion for recognizing that accrual of wealth," that is, the profits capitalized.

42. When discussing the taxation of stock dividends in 1922, Powell said of the taxation of corporate profits, first to the corporation and then to the stockholder:

> In assessing these two taxes no attention is paid to the actual situation. . . . In approving of this neglect the Supreme Court reveals the miraculous properties of incorporation.

He went on to say that those who do not worship the corporate entity as a real presence but "regard a corporation as nothing but a legal device whereby human beings may pool their activities and acquire peculiar legal privileges and duties must in their realism realize how very peculiar these peculiar privileges and duties may be."

43. Probably the decisions and dicta quoted should not be regarded as bearing on the broad question of unrealized appreciation, but only on the narrower special case in which appreciation is due to retention of realized profits by corporations.

44. As income taxation becomes more onerous, the need for care in defining income grows in importance. And today, for the same reason, methods of determining taxable income in turn require consideration in deciding how income—and particularly business income—shall be determined for other purposes.

Gross Income

45. The confusion caused by the varied senses in which the word "income" is used is aggravated by the common misuse of the expression "gross income." The expression has a legitimate use to describe an aggregate of income on which there are a number of claimants, and the deduction therefrom of the portion due or accruing to one party will leave a balance of net income inuring to the benefit of another or others. This use is illustrated in the Institute's *Accounting Research Bulletin* No. 9, page 73:

Sales
    Less cost of sales

Gross income
    Deduct expenses

Net income from sales
    Deduct bond interest

Net income of corporation
    Preferred dividends

Net income for common stock

Some would favor inserting another heading, "Net income before income tax," but others would oppose it.

46. The meaning of the term "gross income" as used in the Revenue Acts has often been misconstrued by courts and others as including gross sales. The Supreme Court avoided this misconception in the important case of *Doyle* v. *Mitchell Brothers Co., 247* U.S. 179 (1918).

47. In that case the Government had contended that the gross proceeds of sale were income, and that only such deductions could be made from such "income" as were expressly permitted by law. The Court, however, took the position that only the gain from sales was income. The cost of property sold or other costs which had to be incurred to produce the revenues must be deducted from proceeds of sales even though there was no explicit provision of the law permitting those deductions. The soundness and importance of this decision have been fully recognized by accountants, but have often been lost to sight in legal briefs and court rulings on taxation. The point involved is of cardinal significance in the consideration of accounting concepts of income.

48. In "national income" statistics the term "gross national product" is used to mean roughly the aggregate of net income and capital consumption (depreciation and related charges).

49. The facts that income exists only by definition, that in common use the word is employed in materially different senses, and that the "income" for a given period may properly vary with the purpose or entity for which it is being determined, make it desirable that the word

should be used with a qualification or explanation which will indicate the purpose and viewpoint clearly.

50. The income derived from business operations, for instance, may be viewed from the standpoint of the enterprise, the corporation which is carrying on the enterprise, the individual stockholder of the corporation (to whom the price that he paid for his stock is a relevant factor), or from that of the national economy.

51. Again, income may be measured, or expressed, in a variety of ways. It may be *conceived* in terms of a particular currency without regard to changes in value of that currency, or in terms of a less unstable unit. However conceived, it may be *expressed* (either initially or by a process of conversion through the use of indexes) in terms of any given currency or even in a conceptual unit, such as the "unit of gold" which is used by the Bank for International Settlements.

52. Manifestly, there is great convenience in adopting a unit that is widely employed, and for any country the national currency is, obviously by far, the most convenient and useful unit. But it is desirable constantly to keep in mind that the monetary unit is designed primarily for use as a medium of exchange, and that its secondary use as an accounting symbol is only an expedient. In accounting the monetary unit is a tool or symbol whose character should always be kept in mind in determining the manner of its use, and which may have to be discarded if it loses the characteristics which make it useful.

SECTION 3

Business Income and Accounting

1. Business, like income, is a word that conveys a general idea rather than a precise meaning. Whether a course of action constitutes carrying on a business depends largely on motivation, which cannot be judged except by what is actually done. A collector may at first be intent on acquisition. Later he may seek to cull out and improve his collection, and perhaps to profit from his acquired knowledge by an occasional purchase and resale. At some point his hobby may become a business.

2. It may be assumed that the task of implementing any concept of business income is essentially an accounting task, but it must always be borne in mind that income and categories related to it "are not logical categories at all; they are rough approximations, used by the businessman to steer himself through the bewildering changes of situation which confront him." [1]

3. It will be useful to consider first what income is in relation to certain types of enterprises which are admittedly of a business nature. Among these a common and significant distinction lies between manufacturing or trading enterprises and financial concerns. In practice an important distinction also is that between enterprises which are assumed to have an indefinite life and those whose prospective life is subject to a natural limitation that materially affects the measurement of their income.

Corporations

4. Corporations may be subdivided into those whose capital stock is widely held and freely transferable (broadly speaking, those whose securities are listed on stock markets) and the corporations, typically smaller, in which management and investment are closely combined.

[1] J. R. Hicks, *Value and Capital,* 2nd ed. (The Clarendon Press, 1946), p. 171.

Another significant distinction is between utilities subject to regulation and other business enterprises.

5. In the following discussion consideration will be given first, and principally, to the problem of deciding what is the "business income" of corporations (1) whose accounting is conducted on the assumption that their future life will be indefinitely long, (2) which are engaged in the business of buying or producing and selling goods or services, and (3) whose managements are not closely identified with ownership, the latter being in the form of securities which are readily transferable and are held largely by persons who have no responsibility for, or means of knowledge of, the detailed operations and the accounting methods of the corporation.

6. The discussion will be directed to the *financial accounting* of such companies, by which is meant the accounting that is designed to summarize financial results, not only for the use of management, but also for the use or benefit of persons who are not actively associated with the business, who therefore do not have access to the underlying information, and must rely upon reports made for them by management. This point is important because in recent times there have been developing differences between the bases of financial accounting and "administrative accounting" that provides information for the use and guidance of those charged with executive responsibility and policy.

7. Of corporations that carry on the enterprises that are of greatest public importance, some are organized under special charters (such as railroads, utilities, banks, and so forth) and some under general corporation laws. This being so, any study of business income involves, as a practical matter, consideration of the nature of corporations as well as of the definition of business income. The corporation is a creation of the State with rights, privileges, immunities, and obligations which vary from State to State. Even more significant for present purposes is its many-sided character.

8. Indeed, the question, What is the business income for a year of a corporation, is one that may be said to bear a fairly close analogy to the question, What is the color of the chameleon? For income, like

color, is dependent on external conditions, and a matter of imperceptible gradations from one extreme to another. And the corporation has in relation to income an even greater capacity for adaptation than the chameleon has in relation to color. A corporation is at one and the same time a person, an association of persons, and the shell of an enterprise, or a part of the framework of a system. Through legal devices, such as reorganization, its income determination may be radically changed without any change in the external operations. By merger it may undergo a mystical union so that it becomes a continuation of its former self and also of a number of corporations once unrelated.

9. So protean is its nature that the courts have been compelled to assert the right at any time to look through it to the enterprise which it carries on, to its ownership, or to other relations.

10. At one time the stockholders of general business corporations were permitted within wide limits to define profits or income for corporate purposes to suit themselves; but the corporation is a creation of law, and the law has always the right to define the sense in which the word "income" shall be used by those who take advantage of its creation. Ultimately, therefore, the definition of income may become a political question, and be determined by the attitude of legislators toward savings, industrial growth, and so forth. No study of this aspect of the problem has been undertaken by the Group.

Fundamentals of Income Accounting

11. The Committee on Accounting Procedure of the American Institute of Accountants adopted in 1938 the view that, "A fair determination of income for successive accounting periods is the most important single purpose of the general accounting reports of a corporation." Today it might be said that the effects of inflation on the corporation are of comparable importance.

12. Income accounting necessarily rests on a framework of postulates and assumptions; these are accepted and acceptable as being useful, not as demonstrable truths; their usefulness is always open to reconsideration. Perhaps the three most important of the fundamental postulates generally accepted today are the "monetary postulate," the "postulate

of permanence," and the "realization postulate." The three may be stated as follows:

1. Fluctuations in value of the monetary unit, which is the accounting symbol, may properly be ignored.

2. In the absence of actual evidence to the contrary, the prospective life of the enterprise may be deemed to be indefinitely long.

3. The entire income from sale arises at the moment when realization is deemed to take place.

The Monetary Postulate

13. The postulate that fluctuations in the value of the monetary unit may be ignored is probably the longest established of the three mentioned. From which it follows that income or profit in a given year may arise in part from manufacture or trading, and in part from changes in the value of the monetary unit during the period. The significance of the two types of profit is by no means the same for purposes for which determinations of income or profit are most commonly made.

14. Thorstein Veblen said of this postulate:

. . . among the securely known facts of psychology, as touches the conduct of business, is the ingrained persuasion that the money unit is stable, the value of the money unit being the base-line of business transactions.[2]

In a footnote he said of the presumption:

It is known not to accord with fact, but still it remains a principle of conduct. It has something like an instinctive force; or perhaps rather, it is something like a tropismatic reaction, in that presumption is acted on even when it is known to be misleading.

15. Paton and Littleton said of it, among other things:

The assumption that recorded dollar cost continues to represent actual cost permeates accounting thought and practice, as it does the law. Accounting, in other words, assumes a stable measuring unit. In periods of major price movements this assumption is clearly invalid for certain purposes, as has been pointed out by various writers in recent years. Undoubtedly interpretative accounting faces a challenge at this point.[3]

[2] *Absentee Ownership and Business Enterprise in Recent Times* (Huebsch, 1923), p. 179.
[3] W. A. Paton and A. C. Littleton, *An Introduction to Corporate Accounting Standards* (American Accounting Association Monograph 3, 1940), p. 23.

Postulate of Permanence

16. The postulate of permanence has perhaps the next longest history, though it was originally applied more narrowly than it should be applied today.

17. The more closely the problems of modern accounting are studied, the more apparent become the far-reaching implications of this postulate.

18. Paton and Littleton recognized it as being adopted for convenience, and warned:

> The "going-concern" or continuity concept has an important bearing on periodic reports. In so far as the business enterprise is a continuous stream of activities, with those of the moment conditioned by those of the past and in turn conditioning those of the future, the process of breaking the stream into fiscal segments, for each of which reports are prepared, severs many real connections and tends to give a specious color of immediate reliability to data which in substantial measure depend on the course of future events. It should be recognized that financial statements, even under the most favorable circumstances, are provisional in character; the impressions gained from them and the decisions resting upon them may have to be changed in the light of future events and should be tempered with a knowledge of this contingency.[4]

The Realization Postulate

19. The postulate of realization is of quite modern origin. In America at least its acceptance could not be related back to any date prior to the First World War. It will be discussed in its historical setting hereafter (*infra,* page 23).

20. Two world wars and social developments have brought about fundamental changes in the conditions under which business is conducted. It is part of the purpose of this discussion to consider some effects of these changes on the accounting principles, postulates, or conventions which are, or perhaps should be, widely accepted.

The Origin and Development of Financial Accounting

21. Financial accounting becomes especially necessary when forms of business organization are created in which management and beneficial

[4] *Ibid.,* pp. 9–10.

ownership may be disassociated; it has grown in importance with the development of the private limited liability company. A hundred years ago there were no general laws authorizing the creation of such companies in England, though they had long existed in the United States. In 1855 Cobden, in advocating such a law in England, cited as a model an Iowa statute.

22. The earliest accounting discussion that seems to be significant in relation to our present topic is to be found in Lawrence Robert Dicksee's book *Auditing,* which was published in London in 1892.

23. Henry R. Hatfield, a penetrating commentator on accounting, and an authority on its history, has suggested that modern bookkeeping was one of the products of the Renaissance, but that it made little progress over the next four centuries. He has cited Dicksee and Francis W. Pixley as pioneers in an unprecedented flow of "serious scientific literature" on the subject in England.[5] Elsewhere he has explained the cause: business had become a continuum, so that income had to be allocated to years, where before it had been measured only for completed ventures. Of American texts Hatfield mentioned only Charles Ezra Sprague's *Philosophy of Accounts,* 1907, which was, however, less significant than his own admirable *Modern Accounting* of 1909.

Dicksee and the Postulate of Permanence

24. Dicksee considered three types of organization. First came the parliamentary companies which carried on railway and other public-utility enterprises; next, the private traders whose liability was unlimited, and whose business entities were subject to frequent change through shifts of ownership; and third, the registered companies formed under the Companies Act of 1862. The position of the registered companies he regarded as not yet fully determined.

25. He emphasized that the accounting of the parliamentary companies was based on the assumption of *permanence.* He recognized more clearly than later writers two natural corollaries: first, that the burden to be borne by revenue was that of assuring, as far as possible,

[5] *Journal of Accountancy,* XLIV (1927), pp. 267-268.

permanence of the enterprise (not of its original value), and second, that fluctuations in the value of assets necessary to continuance might be regarded as irrelevant. A third might have been added, that the problem of profits or losses on the termination of an enterprise was left unconsidered.

26. The income of private traders was, he suggested, measured by the change in net worth, due allowance being made for capital paid in or withdrawn.

27. The contrast thus presented might have seemed less striking if he had gone on to consider how the valuations necessary in the case of private traders were commonly made. Some assumption as to the duration of the enterprise was necessary for this purpose. Valuations as well as accounting rested on what has been described as the "going concern" basis, which is more accurately described by Dicksee's term, the assumption of *permanence*.

28. Hence, the presumption of indefinite continuance of the business formed, directly or indirectly, a part of the basis of income determination for businesses other than those of parliamentary companies.

29. Today this presumption of indefinite life is applied, and properly applied, over a wider range than Dicksee contemplated in 1892, and the corollaries should, therefore, receive correspondingly wider recognition. Depreciation accounting, based as it is on an estimate of the useful life of assets, must be regarded as implicitly assuming that the enterprise will endure longer than any unit which is included in that accounting. The problem of income accounting when the assumption of indefinite continuance ceases to be valid requires more consideration than it has hitherto received.

Emergence of the Realization Postulate

30. A review of accounting, legal, and economic literature suggests that the realization postulate was not accepted prior to the First World War. In 1913 leading authorities in all these fields in Great Britain and America seemed to agree on the "increase in net worth" concept of income (except in the case of "permanent" enterprises), though the way in which it could best be implemented was not settled, and un-

realized appreciation was not perhaps deemed to be a part of "income from operations."

31. Three quotations on this broad question must suffice. In the *Spanish Prospecting Co.* case (1911), 1 Ch. 92, Lord Justice Fletcher Moulton (discussing the question broadly and not in relation to a narrow issue such as the propriety of a dividend) said:

> The word "profits" has in my opinion a well-defined legal meaning, and this meaning coincides with the fundamental conception of "profits" in general parlance, although in mercantile phraseology the word may at times bear meanings indicated by the special context which deviate in some respects from this fundamental signification. "Profits" implies a comparison between the state of a business at two specific dates usually separated by an interval of a year. The fundamental meaning is the amount of gain made by the business during the year. This can only be ascertained by a comparison of the assets of the business at the two dates.

32. In his *Accounting Practice and Procedure* (1913) A. L. Dickinson, who may be regarded as an authority on both English and American accounting, said:

> In the widest possible view, profits may be stated as the realized increment in value of the whole amount invested in an undertaking; and, conversely, loss is the realized decrement in such value. Inasmuch, however, as the ultimate realization of the original investment is from the nature of things deferred for a long period of years, during which partial realizations are continually taking place, it becomes necessary to fall back on estimates of value at certain definite periods, and to consider as profit or loss the estimated increase or decrease between any two such periods.

33. However, he emphasized that unrealized appreciation was not an element in the "income from operations" which was becoming more important as interests in businesses became more widely distributed. Upon this point a report on profits of a corporation prepared by him in 1909 is of special interest. There are shown first the profits from operations for a series of years. To the total of these is added a figure described as "Appreciation of investments during the eight years." Thus, a total is reached which is described as "Total profits." In his book Dickinson said (pages 80–81), "It would be unfair, especially in a young and

657.48 St94c
C.1

growing country to exclude appreciation of capital assets from the accounts."

34. Robert H. Montgomery, whose editions of *Auditing* form a useful guide to change of accounting thought, recognized the "increase in net worth" concept as acceptable in principle, though generally impracticable, as late as the 1927 edition (page 360).

35. Alfred Marshall in his *Principles of Economics,* first published in 1890, had said:

> When a man is engaged in business, his profits for the year are the excess of his receipts from his business during the year over his outlay for his business; the difference between the value of his stock and plant at the end and at the beginning of the year being taken as part of his receipts or as part of his outlay, according as there has been an increase or a decrease of value.

Summary of Position in 1913

36. It may be said that prior to World War I the monetary postulate was virtually unquestioned, the postulate of permanence was accepted to a limited but increasing extent, and the realization postulate and the related "cost principle" were not a part of the accepted doctrine.

37. Some misconceptions on this last point have arisen from the fact that cost was often used as the best or conservative measure of value in a period when prices generally were rising, as they were during the early years of the present century. The transition to the idea that cost was used *as such* was easy.

The Effect of the Sixteenth Amendment on Accounting Postulates

38. In American accounting a profound effect on the concepts of income was created by the adoption in 1913 of a constitutional amendment authorizing the Congress to levy without apportionment among the states a tax on income from whatever source derived, and by the imposition of such taxes on a large scale during World War I. The corporation excise tax law of 1909 had been levied nominally on the basis of receipts and payments in respect of income. This quite impracticable basis was adopted, despite the protests of accountants, for reasons which were said by some to be of a constitutional or legal nature. As late as

1918 the question whether there was power to tax what had not been realized in cash was being discussed. In the interval the practical difficulties presented by the law of 1909 and the early income tax laws had been overcome by regulations or permissive provisions in the law that were so convenient to taxpayers as to be generally adopted. Gradually there emerged the concepts of "the completed transaction" and "cash or its equivalent"—which became embodied in the law of 1918.

39. In interpreting the amendment, as applied to the taxation of individuals, the Supreme Court declined to be bound by accounting or economic concepts of income. It held that the word "income" must be construed in accordance with popular usage, and that when so used it connoted something severed from capital. The Court defined income as the gain derived from capital, from labor, or from both combined; but, as Roswell Magill put it, it laid even more stress on severance than on gain. There could be no gain without severance, or, in other words, without a realization.

40. Discussing the realization postulate, George O. May has said:

Manifestly, when a laborious process of manufacture and sale culminates in the delivery of the product at a profit, that profit is not attributable, except conventionally, to the moment when the sale or delivery occurred. The accounting convention which results in such an attribution is justified only by its demonstrated practical usefulness.

It is instructive to consider how it happens that such a rule produces results that are practically useful and reliable. The explanation is, that in the normal business there are at any one moment transactions at every stage of the production of profit, from beginning to end. If the distribution were exactly uniform, an allocation of income according to the proportion of completion of each unit would produce the same result as the attribution of the entire profit to the final step of sale.

A number of conclusions immediately suggest themselves: first, that the convention is valid for the greatest variety of purposes where the flow of product is most nearly uniform; second, that it is likely to be more generally valid for a longer than for a shorter period; and, third, that its applicability is open to serious question (at least for some purposes) where the final consummation is irregular in time and in amount. Thus, the rule is almost completely valid in regard to a business which is turning out a standard product in relatively small units at a reasonably stable rate of production. It is less generally valid—or, to put it otherwise, the figure of profit reached is less generally significant—in the case of a company engaged in building large units, such as battleships, or carrying out construction contracts.

These considerations throw a useful light on the problem of the varying uses of accounts; they also explain a tendency which has been notable during the last fifty years in the accounting treatment of large contracts and similar enterprises. In earlier days, when the use of accounts as an indication of earning capacity was not considered so important, when income taxes, if any, were small, and when conservatism was regarded as a virtue, the procedure of treating the gain on even a large contract as arising at the moment of its completion was unobjectionable. Any other method might have resulted in taking credit for a profit that might never be earned. In recent years there has developed a much greater readiness to take credit for profits on uncompleted transactions, in order to secure a more realistic allocation, and a more useful guide to earning capacity.[6]

41. The Supreme Court held, as already noted, that gains on the sale or severance of capital assets might be taxed as income. In view of the great rise in prices that took place between 1913 and 1920, the realization postulate was perhaps necessary if only to moderate the effects of holding that gain included a gain that represented only decline in the value of the monetary unit. The accounting validity of the Court's position did not go unquestioned, especially during the pri rise of the war and postwar period, and ways were found of excludii "gains" of this type from determinations of income, but interest in the subject waned after the violent price decline of 1920–1921.

42. The assertion by the Court of the realization postulate lent support to the proposition that, until realized, assets should be carried at cost, and thus contributed to the building up in accounting literature of a so-called "traditional cost principle."

43. The displacement of the "increase in net worth" test of income by the "realization" test made income determination an accounting problem rather than one of inventory and valuation. It became necessary to distinguish the charges to be deducted from gross sales, in order to arrive at the gain that was gross income, from those that had to be deducted from gross income to determine net income. This dis-

[6] *Financial Accounting* (Macmillan, 1943), pp. 30–31; slightly revised.

tinction between "product costs" and "period costs" is of fundamental importance in accounting determinations of income. It is, however, often obscured in accounting texts.

Matching Costs and Revenues

44. With the change from "increased net worth" to the "realization" test of income, it became common to speak of income determination as being essentially a process of "matching costs and revenues." This practice has found strong support in academic accounting circles.

45. Thus discussing concepts, Paton and Littleton, after pointing out that "portrayals in financial statements must be recognized as provisional in character," said in 1940:

> With acquisition and disposition prices measuring both the efforts to produce results and the results produced, the principal concern of accounting is the periodic matching of costs and revenues as a test-reading by which to gauge the effect of the efforts expended.[7]

The cardinal virtue claimed for the principle of matching costs and revenues is that it results in determinations that are objective and verifiable. Paton and Littleton defined objective evidence as "evidence which is impersonal and external to the person most concerned." They conceded that "acounting facts are not always conclusively objective or completely verifiable," but said that "observers are of the opinion that accounting facts are more convincingly objective now than they used to be and more definitely verifiable." [8]

46. Only in part are costs "matched" against revenues, and "matching" gives an inadequate indication of what is actually done. One defect of the statement is that it obscures essential differences in the nature of the various charges that must be met out of revenues before net income is determined.

Classification of Charges Against Revenue

47. The lines between classes of costs or charges against revenues cannot be sharply drawn, but in broad outline (which is all that is

[7] *An Introduction to Corporate Accounting Standards* (American Accounting Association Monograph 3, 1940), p. 7.
[8] *Ibid.,* p. 19.

necessary for consideration of *concepts*) they fall into two categories: *product costs* and *period costs*. The former are charged as the product is delivered (or the service is rendered), the latter as the period to which they are deemed applicable passes. This being so, it would be more accurate to describe income determination as a process of (1) matching product costs against revenues, and (2) allocating other costs to periods.

48. Even this description might have to be modified to take cognizance of such procedures as the use of "cost or market, whichever is lower," as the basis of inventorying, one of the oldest and most widely employed of accounting methods. In England the reduction to market value is regarded as a provision for an anticipated loss made out of realized profits.[9] In the United States the reduction is regarded as an element in determining profit.

49. Some accountants, particularly in the academic field, have advocated rejection of the "cost or market" basis. It is said to be illogical to take cognizance of a fall in value in determining income or profit while ignoring a rise. Practicing accountants generally, however, continue to favor the method. In recent years efforts have been made to secure harmony by stating as the guiding principle that only "useful" costs should be carried forward in inventories, and by agreeing that costs which cannot reasonably be expected to be recovered are no longer useful.

50. A point that is significant for the present purpose is that two different theoretical problems are presented by (*a*) a fall in value which merely keeps pace with the change in the general price level and (*b*) a fall relative to other prices.

51. When the subject is studied, it soon becomes apparent that *what* transactions or *what* "acquisition prices" shall govern the determination is a matter either of convention or of subjective choice; hence income determination is by no means as objective or as factual a process as one might be led to suppose.

52. One consequence of the emphasis on the word "cost," without clear identification of the cost that is relevant, is that changes in substance are more easily brought about by widening the definition of "cost" than by frank admission of a substantial change of basis. The

[9] See *Recommendation* No. X of the Institute of Chartered Accountants.

adoption of "LIFO cost" and the gradual change in the interpretation of the term illustrate the point. This tendency is, of course, often found in law and other disciplines. Mr. Justice Holmes speaks of the development of law as being a process in which "fictions" are carried to the point at which the results become too manifestly absurd and good sense overcomes the tendency.[10] LIFO has been developed to the point at which the fiction that it is a cost method may have to be abandoned.

53. A natural subclassification of either "product costs" or "period costs" may be based on the *time relation* between the incurring of the cost or expense and the time when it is to be brought into account in determining income. There may be:

a) no interval, in which case the cost or expense will never be treated as an asset;

b) a short postponement, in which case the cost or expense will be carried either as "stock in trade" (or inventory) or as a "deferred charge";

c) a long postponement, in which case the cost may be carried as a capital asset, to be distributed usually by a systematic procedure over a series of periods;

d) an anticipation, in which case a "provision" for the future cost or expense will be carried on the "liability" side of the balance sheet.[11]

The Cost Principle—What Costs?

54. As a result of the development of the concepts of "matching costs and revenues" and of the "cost principle," accounting has often been represented by accountants and regulatory authorities as being simpler and more factual than it can possibly be.

55. Indeed, in 1949 a leading article in the *Accountant,* London, went so far as to say that up to that date accounting had been a matter of recording, and that the function of the accountant was analogous to that of the scorekeeper in a cricket match. Obviously, however, he discharges also some of the functions of the umpire.

[10] *Collected Legal Papers* (1920), p. 101.

[11] A discussion of this problem is contained in the monograph *Business Income and Price Levels: An Accounting Study,* published by the Study Group in 1949.

56. One major phase of the crucial issue "What costs are relevant?" presents the question whether it shall be the cost of what is disposed of or the cost of replacing it—actual or estimated. This is a phase to which the Group decided to direct particular attention.

57. Three main schools of thought have existed. *The first,* reflected in the classifications of the Federal Power Commission and Federal Communications Commission, and to a lesser extent in that of the Interstate Commerce Commission, leads to the result that the charge should be the oldest cost that can be deemed relevant.

58. *The second,* reflected in the double-account system of English utilities and LIFO accounting, is that it should be the most recent cost that can be deemed relevant.

59. *The third,* reflected in general accounting practice, is that the choice is based "partly on theoretical and partly on practical considerations" (to use the language of the report to the Stock Exchange in 1932, *supra*), and that considerable freedom of election should be permitted.

60. The first method *maximizes* and the second *minimizes* the reflection of changes of price level in income determination, while the third may be said to be neutral on this point.

61. When costs are closely scrutinized, it becomes apparent that there are relatively few cases in which the cost, or the portion of a cost, which ought to be charged against particular revenues or a particular period can be determined on a purely factual basis or without applying any accounting convention. Moreover, where physical identification and a strictly factual determination are possible, accounting sometimes rejects that basis because of the opportunity for manipulation that its acceptance might create.

Criteria of Classification

62. In general accounting the decision whether cost or expense shall be charged against revenues as soon as incurred does not by any means turn wholly on whether the benefits from it are expected to be short- or long-lived. Other factors considered in practice are whether the expenditure is made for a tangible or an intangible consideration; whether the period of usefulness can be estimated with some measure of assurance; or even the element of practicability.

63. For present purposes the most important points are that various costs of intangibles are apt to be charged off as incurred, and that partial replacements of physical assets (repairs and renewals) may or may not be charged immediately according to the general method of accounting applied to the property a part of which is replaced. Thus expenditure for a machine with a life of three years, which replaces one scrapped and which costs $1,000, may be passed through a capital asset account and distributed over the three years, but a repainting job costing $5,000 and expected to last five years may be charged off immediately.

Regulated Accounting and "Original Cost"

64. The doctrine of the "cost principle" was stimulated and a new variant developed during the 1930's by the course of events in the regulation of rates of charges for service of public utilities on the basis of the cost of the service and a return on investment.

65. For a quarter of a century prior to 1897 the general trend of prices had been downward. In that year they reached the lowest point since 1750. This decline, and the reduction in the physical difficulties of railroad construction, led shippers to advance the claim that the railroads were not entitled to a return on their investment cost, but only on the current fair value of their property. The Supreme Court adopted this view (at least in dicta) in *Smythe* v. *Ames* in 1898.

66. In the early years of the present century, however, prices and land values were rising; in 1913 the wholesale price index was 50 per cent higher than in 1897. The position was reversed. After the further rise in prices that resulted from World War I, the newer utilities—electric light and power, telephone, and so forth—fought vigorously against the regulatory commissions that had been created in many States, and sought to sustain the position taken by the Court in *Smythe* v. *Ames.* For a decade their efforts were successful, the high-water mark being reached in the case of *United Railway & Electric Co. of Baltimore* v. *West,* 280 U.S. 234 (1930). The Courts held that present value must be the measure of the rate base *and of the charge for exhaustion of property.* The prosperity thus created brought with it great abuses, particularly among public-utility holding companies. There were, however, many who thought the prudent investment approach to

the rate base was sounder and probably in the ultimate interest of both parties, and there were many who disapproved the method of providing for property exhaustion that was commonly employed by some electrical utilities.

67. The administration that came into power in 1933 undertook, through Federal Commissions newly created or vested with new powers, the task of breaking up the holding companies and controlling the accounting and financing of the utilities themselves. For a time the Commission sought to justify regulations which were not in harmony with Court decisions as being in conformity with "generally accepted principles of accounting."

This view and some of the specific rules promulgated were strongly opposed by leading accountants. However, as the personnel of the Supreme Court changed, this point became immaterial. The Court took a constantly widening view of the powers of the Commissions, declined to interfere with any regulation unless it could be shown that it was the mere exercise of a whim, and also took a broad view of what was an accounting question.[12]

68. Today a concept of "original cost" (by which is meant cost to the person who first devoted the property to public service) governs the accounting of corporations subject to regulation by the Federal Power Commission or the Federal Communications Commission, and many, if not most, State Commissions. It also influences the thinking of the Securities and Exchange Commission, which has special functions in the utility field.

Accounting Under the Securities Acts of 1933 and 1934

69. Under the same administration the influence of the Federal Government on income determination was extended in another way. By the Securities Acts of 1933 and 1934 (as amended), the Securities and Exchange Commission was given an extensive jurisdiction over accounting in relation to companies whose securities were distributed to the public or traded in upon the exchanges. Not only was the Commission given power to ensure that accounting reports of such companies would be in conformity with accepted accounting principles; there was also con-

[12] Cf. *U.S. et al.* v. *New York Telephone Co.*, 326 U.S. 638, 655 (1946).

ferred on it an original jurisdiction to prescribe to some extent, at least, the methods to be followed and even the rates of depreciation to be adopted.

70. Up to the present the Commission has relied mainly on the first of these powers. In its *Annual Report* for 1950 (page 154) the Commission said:

> Although the statutes administered by the Commission give it wide rule-making power, accounting, based as it is largely upon convention and existing financial business concepts, is of such a nature that the Commission has not yet found it necessary or desirable in most areas to establish extensive accounting rules and regulations dealing with accounting problems.

It no doubt recognizes that a heavy responsibility in respect of statements rests upon the independent accountants who report upon them, whereas it is not regarded as permissible to assert that the Commission has any responsibility for the propriety of the accounts, such as would actually exist if the Commission should undertake to prescribe methods to be adopted, but which might be adopted by corporations only under compulsion.

The Institute, the New York Stock Exchange and the Securities and Exchange Commission

71. The Securities and Exchange Commission has undoubtedly been influenced in the restraint it has displayed by the activities of the American Institute of Accountants and the New York Stock Exchange a year or two before and ever since the introduction of the legislation which became the Securities Acts of 1933 and 1934.

72. In 1930 accounting cooperation in the work of the Exchange was increased by the formal appointment of a special committee of the Institute for that purpose. Thereafter consideration was given not only to specific problems but to the possibility of securing a greater degree of uniformity in practice and a better public understanding of the nature of corporate financial statements. As a result, a far-reaching program was evolved which was set forth in a letter addressed by the Institute's Committee to the Exchange under date of September 22, 1932.[13]

[13] *Audits of Corporate Accounts*, 1934.

73. In this letter the Committee rejected the "increase in net worth" concept of income, and accepted the view that the real value of the assets of any large business is collective and dependent mainly on the earning capacity of the enterprise. It explained the origin of existing accounting practice as follows:

> Some method . . . has to be found by which the proportion of a given expenditure to be charged against the operations in a year, and the proportion to be carried forward, may be determined; otherwise, it would be wholly impossible to present an annual income account. Out of this necessity has grown up a body of conventions, based partly on theoretical and partly on practical considerations, which form the basis for the determination of income and the preparation of balance sheets today. And while there is a fairly general agreement on certain broad principles to be followed in the formulation of conventional methods of accounting, there remains room for differences in the application of those principles which affect the results reached in a very important degree. . . .
>
> Most investors realize today that balance sheets and income accounts are largely the reflection of individual judgments, and that their value is therefore to a large extent dependent on the competence and honesty of the persons exercising the necessary judgment. The importance of method, and particularly of consistency of method from year to year, is by no means equally understood.

The Committee recommended that efforts should be made:

> To emphasize the cardinal importance of the income account, such importance being explained by the fact that the value of a business is dependent mainly on its earning capacity; and to take the position that an annual income account is unsatisfactory unless it is so framed as to constitute the best reflection reasonably obtainable of the earning capacity of the business under the conditions existing during the year to which it relates. . . .
>
> . . . to cause a statement of the methods of accounting and reporting employed by it [the listed corporation] to be formulated in sufficient detail to be a guide to its accounting department . . . to have such statement adopted by its board so as to be binding on its accounting officers; and to furnish such statement to the Exchange and make it available to any stockholder on request and upon payment, if desired, of a reasonable fee.

To secure assurances that the methods so formulated will be followed consistently from year to year and that if any change is made in the principles or any material change in the manner of application, the stockholders and the Exchange shall be advised when the first accounts are presented in which effect is given to such change.

To endeavor to bring about a change in the form of audit certificate so that the auditors would specifically report to the shareholders whether the accounts as presented were properly prepared in accordance with the methods of accounting regularly employed by the company, defined as already indicated.

74. The proposal was warmly approved by the Exchange, by corporations, and by the Controllers Institute, and was made public in pamphlets issued early in 1934.

75. In its final form the proposal contemplated that every accountant's report should state whether the accounting practices established by the company had been followed and whether they were in accordance with accepted accounting principles.

Generally Accepted Principles

76. The Institute immediately created a Committee of seven on the Development of Accounting Principles, consisting of the chairmen of its standing Committees on Accounting Procedure, Education, and Professional Ethics, and of its special Committees on Cooperation with the Securities and Exchange Commission (just created), stock exchanges, investment bankers, and bankers. In its first report this Committee said in part:

> Since principles of accounting cannot be arrived at by pure reasoning, but must find their justification in practical wisdom, the Committee believes that the Institute should proceed with caution in selecting from the methods more or less commonly employed those which should be accorded the standing of principles or accepted rules of accounting.

It recommended that the Institute should seek to secure the aid of bodies possessing higher authority in promoting general acceptance of rules or principles which it might lay down for the guidance of its members.

77. The phrase "in accordance with generally accepted accounting principles, consistently maintained," was adopted as a criterion of the propriety of accounting practices by the Securities and Exchange Commission. The Commission has not, however, up to now required the full scheme of disclosure of methods which was outlined in the recommendations of the Institute's Committee in 1932, and which was an integral part of the procedure contemplated by the Institute and the New York Stock Exchange. Both the Securities and Exchange Commission and the New York Stock Exchange do, of course, require an amount of disclosure that has added greatly to the usefulness of reports to the general public.

78. In the period since the report to the Stock Exchange in 1932, the Institute has made efforts, in cooperation with the Securities and Exchange Commission, to bring about a closer approach to uniformity in accounting for routine transactions, and substantial progress has been made in this direction. However, new problems of major importance have been created by changes of price levels, by higher rates of income tax, by development of new pension obligations based on past service, by new methods of financing, and by new procedures required, or permitted, for tax purposes. These will be discussed later herein (*infra,* page 63 *et seq.*).

Accounting Practices and Income Taxation

79. The Congress has exercised a powerful influence on methods of income determination by laying down rules governing deductions from revenue for income tax purposes, conditioned in some cases on the employment of the same method in the taxpayer's own financial accounting.

80. Of these provisions, those which in 1938 and 1939 authorized the use of the last-in, first-out (LIFO) method of inventorying have been of great practical significance and are particularly interesting in relation to the subject matter of this report. More recently the rules relating to pensions have exerted an even greater influence on corporate income accounting.

81. Our first carefully drawn Income Tax Law (that of 1918) and all later laws provide that taxable business income shall normally be

determined by the methods ordinarily employed by the taxpayer in keeping his books and accounts. In this our law followed, and was influenced by, the long-established practice in England indicated by the following quotation taken from a departmental report:

> There is, so far as we are aware, no statutory definition of "profits." Mr. Clark, the official witness from the Inland Revenue, in his evidence before us, referred to three cases. The Sun Insurance Company v. Clark, which went to the House of Lords. Smith v. The Lion Brewery Company, and the Usher Brewery case. In the first case Lord Moulton used the words "we have it by our own reasoning and I think by the *action of all commercial men* that the proper way to ascertain profits . . ."
>
> Lord Justice Farwell in the second case said, "the expression 'Profit of a trade' bears its ordinary signification as used by businessmen in business."
>
> In the third case Lord Loreburn said "profits and gains must be estimated on ordinary principles of commercial trade." All these three dicta base the ascertainment of profits on commercial practice. And it appears that in the absence of a statutory definition the Board of Inland Revenue has felt itself unable to contest the base stock system of valuation where it has prevailed.[14]

(It will be observed that the language of Lord Justice Fletcher Moulton (quoted in Paragraph 31) was not cited.)

82. These precedents reinforced argument based on convenience, and led to congressional adoption of Section 212(*b*) of the Act of 1918, which provides:

> The net income shall be computed upon the basis of the taxpayer's annual accounting period (fiscal year or calendar year as the case may be) *in accordance with the method of accounting regularly employed in keeping the books of such taxpayer;* but if no such method of accounting has been so employed, or if the method employed does not clearly reflect the income, the computation shall be made *upon such basis and in such manner as in the opinion of the Commissioner does clearly reflect the income.*[15]

[14] Ministry of Reconstruction, Committee on Financial Risks Attaching to the Holding of Trading Stocks, 1919 Cd 9224, England.
[15] Now Sec. 41 of the Code.

In American practice in recent years, arguments relating to the second part of the clause have led the courts to reject methods commonly employed, but these decisions have been vexatious rather than of great moment. The legislative authorization of LIFO was, however, a highly significant development.

LIFO (*Last-in, First-out*)

83. The development of LIFO is a chapter of great importance in the history of accounting thought in America.

84. An express authorization of the use of the LIFO method in certain cases was written into our tax law in 1938. It appears that this was done in order to overcome administrative rejection of it, though responsible members of the Congress had expressed the view that it was authorized by the then existing law.

85. The origin of the proposal itself, and the first expression of opinion upon it by an official accounting body in America are set forth in the following quotation from a report of a special committee of the American Institute of Accountants in 1936:

> The prime purpose of the "last-in, first-out" principle, which the board of directors of the American Petroleum Institute has recommended to the membership of that Institute, is to bring about, in the determination of profits in the financial accounts, a substantial correlation between sales prices and those raw material prices which have been directly causative of such sales prices.
>
> In its practical effect in the accomplishment of this objective, the "last-in, first-out" principle may be viewed as comparable to the "base stock" or "basic inventory" method of inventory valuation, the purpose of which likewise is that the revenue from high sales prices be burdened with the costs causative of such high sales prices, and not leave high price level inventories to be absorbed later by revenue representing a lower price level, upon the turn of the economic cycle.[16]

86. In 1938, and again in 1939, the Congress approved the use of the method for tax purposes, and in doing so described it as a method of determining *cost*. This designation was apparently adopted to minimize

---

[16] *Year Book* (1936), p. 463.

the extent of the change from existing rules that was involved; it has given rise to misconceptions.

87. The proposal was regarded by some (though not all) of its supporters as a step toward recognition in accounting of the business cycle —the more or less rhythmic succession of periods of activity and recession, which was exercising a strong influence at the time as a result of the studies of the late Wesley C. Mitchell and others.

88. The inventory depression of 1920–1921, and the drastic fall of prices between 1929 and 1932 had raised doubts concerning the practical wisdom of the "cost or market" basis of inventorying which obviously accentuates the swings. The emphasis in accounting, moreover, was shifting from the balance sheet to the income statement. Before World War I the orthodox view was that the inventory was to be conservatively valued and brought into account to determine income. By 1932 the thought was developing that the first need was to measure income, and that the inventory carried forward was a residual. This view was reflected fully in the Institute's *Accounting Research Bulletin* No. 29 (1947).

89. In its *Statement of Accounting Concepts and Standards Underlying Corporate Financial Statements* (1948 revision) the American Accounting Association said:

> For purposes of determining the expense of a period, it is acceptable to assume a flow of the cost of inventoriable items, for example, "first-in, first-out." The residual cost should be carried forward in the balance sheet for assignment in future periods except when it is evident that the cost of an item of inventory cannot be recovered, whether from damage, deterioration, obsolescence, style change, over-supply, reduction in price levels, or other cause. In such event the inventory item should be stated at the estimated amount of sales proceeds less direct expense of completion and disposal. This concept of residual cost may be applied to inventory items, a group of inventory items, or to total inventory. The method of inventory costing should be consistent from period to period and should conform reasonably with practices established within the industry or trade.

The statement did not expressly approve or reject the LIFO method.

90. The only bulletin dealing with inventory pricing that has been

issued by the Committee on Accounting Procedure is *Accounting Research Bulletin* No. 29, July, 1947. The Committee mentioned LIFO in Statement 4 and in the discussion thereof, which are here quoted:

Statement 4—Cost for inventory purposes may be determined under any one of several assumptions as to the flow of cost factors (such as "first-in, first-out," "average," and "last-in, first-out"); the major objective in selecting a method should be to choose the one which, under the circumstances, most clearly reflects periodic income.

The cost to be matched against revenue from a sale may not be the identified cost of the specific item which is sold, especially in cases in which similar goods are purchased at different times and at different prices. Ordinarily, under those circumstances, the identity of goods is lost between the time of acquisition and the time of sale. In any event, if the materials purchased in various lots are identical and interchangeable, the use of identified cost of the various lots may not produce the most useful financial statements. This fact has resulted in the development and general acceptance of several assumptions with respect to the flow of cost factors to provide practical bases for the measurement of periodic income. These methods recognize the variations which exist in the relationships of costs to sales prices under different economic conditions. Thus, where sales prices are promptly influenced by changes in reproductive costs, an assumption of the "last-in, first-out" flow of cost factors may be the more appropriate. Where no such cost-price relationship exists, the "first-in, first-out" or an "average" method may be more properly utilized. . . . In some cases, the business operations may be such as to make it desirable to apply one of the acceptable methods of determining cost to one portion of the inventory or components thereof and another of the acceptable methods to other portions of the inventory.

Although selection of the method should be made on the basis of the individual circumstances, it is obvious that financial statements will be more useful if uniform methods of inventory pricing are adopted by all companies within a given industry.

91. In practice, however, the nature of the business has come to have little or nothing to do with decisions whether LIFO should or should not be adopted.

Extent of Use and Effect of LIFO

92. According to *Accounting Trends and Techniques* published by
the Institute, 98 of 525 companies studied made some use of LIFO in
1949. Of these, 49 of 100 companies were in five groups. In order of
extent of use, the groups were: Petroleum, 60.7 per cent; Meat Products,
58.3 per cent; Metals, 56.7 per cent; Textiles, 53.8 per cent, and Retail,
29 per cent. These figures certainly indicate no pattern of conformity to
Statement 4 of *Accounting Research Bulletin* No. 29. Annual reports
for 1950 reveal a great extension of the use of the LIFO method, with
important effects on reported income.

Thus a textile company stated that it had adopted LIFO in 1950,
and that if the inventories "had been stated as heretofore on the FIFO
(first-in, first-out) basis their stated value would have been increased
by approximately $6,034,000 with a consequent increase of approxi-
mately $2,965,000 in the federal and state income taxes for the
year." The reported income would, of course, have been increased by
$3,069,000 over the reported figure of $6,127,055. The effect of different
methods of accounting for periods of less than a year is strikingly illustrated by the same company's report for the first quarter of 1951. On the
LIFO basis a loss was reported, as compared with a profit of over $2
million in the corresponding quarter of 1950 on a FIFO basis; apparently a larger profit would have been shown in the first quarter of 1951
had the FIFO method been adhered to.

93. The Department of Commerce computes estimates of corporate
profits as reported by the corporations, and estimates the adjustment
necessary to place the computation on the basis of stating charges
against revenues in respect of inventoriable costs at current price levels.
The Department has estimated the adjustment for 1950 at minus $5.1
billion as compared with plus $2.1 billion in 1949. On the unadjusted
basis the profits before taxes were $40.3 billion in 1950 and $27.5
billion in 1949. Adjusted they were $35.2 billion and $29.6 billion,
respectively.[17] The Department has commented:

> The corporate profits component of national income, inclusive of the
> inventory valuation adjustment, rose from $30 billion in 1949 to $35
> billion last year. . . .

[17] *National Income*, 1951 Ed., Table 7, p. 153.

Reported profits before inventory valuation adjustments and before tax, showed a decidedly more pronounced increase, with the 1950 total of $40 billion more than 40 percent larger than that of the previous year. This movement, however, reflected to a large extent the predominant corporate practice of charging inventories to cost-of-sales in terms of book values representing prior-period costs, rather than in terms of current replacement costs. The result of this practice has been to include in reported profits before tax in 1950, when inventory replacement costs were rising rapidly, very large amounts of inventory profits, in contrast to the substantial inventory losses included in 1949 under the opposite condition of falling replacement prices. It is this inventory profit or loss which is eliminated by addition of the inventory valuation adjustment to reported profits in order to secure a measure of earnings from current production appropriate for inclusion in national income.[18]

LIFO as a Concept of "Past Costs"

94. The notion of a number of "assumptions as to the *flow of cost factors*" introduced in *Accounting Research Bulletin* No. 29 may be regarded as an innovation in the field of accounting thought, which was no doubt related to the tax treatment of LIFO as a "cost" concept. The older assumptions, of which FIFO was typical, were based on consideration of a natural flow of goods. Actual flow was not accepted as controlling or perhaps even acceptable, in part because of the difficulty of determining it, but more because of the dangers of manipulation that its acceptance would have created. FIFO was regarded as broadly in harmony with the facts: the latest purchase would normally be made with future demands in mind, and the older goods would be consumed or used first. FIFO or Average Cost thus combined actuality, convenience, and objectivity in a common-sense manner.

95. In the first instance LIFO was accepted for tax purposes in only a limited number of cases and under rigid restrictions. Today the authorization has been greatly extended. The most significant facet of the extension for our present purpose is that which permits its application to *dollar amounts* of inventories on the basis of *price indexes*. This acceptance of indexes is in marked contrast with the refusal to counte-

[18] *Ibid.*, p. 10

nance their use in the determination of charges for exhaustion or consumption of capital assets.

96. The LIFO method is, in many respects, similar to the base-stock method, which has long been employed, to a very limited extent, in financial accounting, but was rejected for tax purposes by the authorities during World War I. The presumption of "permanence" forms an important part of the reasoning by which both are justified, and the use of either implies rejection of the concept of income as the increase in net worth. The amount charged against revenue under LIFO may be the cost (or even the quoted price) of goods (such as raw materials purchased at a foreign port and still there) which could not possibly have been used in production, but which replace, not necessarily with identical goods, materials that have been used. It may not be the cost of any goods actually purchased, but may be determined by a price index. The amount carried forward as inventory may not be the cost of anything that is, or might conceivably be deemed to be, on hand, but the cost of something that has been many times replaced.

Emergency Facilities and Accelerated Depreciation

97. One other development affecting tax accounting should perhaps be mentioned here. World War II led to demands for greatly increased productive facilities, and in some cases there were grave doubts about their postwar usefulness. This was particularly true of the steel industry, which had operated during the decade of the thirties on an average of less than 50 per cent of capacity. Laws were enacted which permitted the amortization of the cost of "emergency facilities" over a period of five years or less by charges that were allowable deductions for income tax purposes. Actually, the demand for products in many cases continued unabated after amortization had been completed.

98. In November, 1946, the Committee on Accounting Procedure, with six members dissenting, issued *Accounting Research Bulletin* No. 27, in which it approved in certain circumstances the restoration on the books of values so written off.

99. The fact that charges for exhaustion that proved to be excessive had been made against revenues, in financial accounting as well as for

tax purposes, undoubtedly influenced the attitude of many accountants and others who opposed any change in the postwar treatment of depreciation.

100. The issue of emergency certificates has recently been resumed on a large scale, but on a basis which may generally not permit full amortization of cost over a five-year period. At a recent congressional hearing it was stated that emergency certificates were issued during World War II in a total amount of $7.5 billion. Since the Korean invasion certificates of a similar though not identical character have been issued to about the same extent.

101. A Treasury report prepared in 1948 and made available to the Group estimated depreciable property at $150 billion and aggregate depreciation charges at $5 billion for corporate and $2.5 billion for noncorporate taxpayers. Possibly 30 to 35 per cent of these totals would relate to property, such as motor equipment, machine tools, and so forth, of relatively short life, and it would seem unlikely that the average rate on property subject to accelerated amortization would normally be more than 4 per cent. On this assumption the acceleration over the full five years would be about $6 billion, or $1.2 billion per annum in the case of certificates issued during the war, and a somewhat smaller sum in respect of those already issued under the existing emergency program.

National Income, 1951 edition, estimates of depreciation allowance for 1947 are as follows:

	Billion
Corporate business	5.28
Noncorporate business, excluding farm and real estate industries	1.53
Real estate industry	2.94
Farm industry	2.11
(Exhibit 35, p. 138)	

The same report estimates the amount of producers' durable equipment charged to current expense for the year 1939 at $1.3 billion (Exhibit 36, p. 140).

Appraisal of Postulates

102. These figures may be compared with estimates of total corporation depreciation allowances for the years 1946 to 1950, made in a publication of the Committee on Economic Development, which are as follows:

	Billion
1946	$4.3
1947	5.2
1948	6.0
1949	6.7
1950	7.1

103. This brief survey may well conclude with an appraisal of the three postulates which have been put forward as the most important part of the framework of accounting assumptions.

104. The *postulate of permanence* seems to be almost completely valid over a wide and increasing area. It is in harmony with the assumption applied in measuring income of individuals: the life expectancy both of human beings and of enterprises that survive infancy is lengthening. Many of our enterprises have reached their fiftieth year of existence or have even longer records. At 6 per cent the present value of an annuity for fifty years is only about 5 per cent less than that of a perpetuity. Large enterprises may have to be reorganized, but they are seldom liquidated. Even when liquidation would be advantageous to stockholders there are various pressures that tend toward continuance of operations.

105. Stated in the form in which it is often presented—that accounting assumes the stability of the monetary unit—the *monetary postulate* is an obvious fiction. Some have sought to strengthen its position by making it a part of the definition of income. Apart from definition it may be justified as one of those fictions that are acceptable because they produce more useful results than can be secured by adoption of a different assumption. The question that arises is whether this is still true.

106. The *realization postulate* may be regarded in the same way and, so considered, is acceptable by reason of its relative certainty, ob-

jectivity, and convenience, although in theory an accrual method might be superior. An admitted defect is that, apart from routine transactions, it may make income too dependent on decisions to take, or refrain from taking, a given action. It is, however, an inherent characteristic of income determinations that they are to a substantial degree subjective, whether decisions rest with managements, stockholders, regulatory bodies, or others.

107. Points that emerge from these considerations are: (*a*) no special reservations are necessary in regard to acceptance of the postulate of permanence in the large area in which its use has public importance, (*b*) some reservation and some alternative determination to the application of the realization postulate may be called for in respect of extraordinary transactions, and (*c*) there is need for either revision of present practice or presentation of alternative determinations in respect of the monetary postulate.

SECTION 4

Specific Problems Considered

1. With the background outlined, we turn to consideration of three specific questions which in 1947 the Group decided to study. The first of these was: "Is LIFO accounting, as now applied, only a reasonable assumption as to the actual flow of goods and costs, or more broadly, a means of bringing costs into account on approximately the same price level as revenues?"

2. It is apparent that LIFO has been advocated or adopted for a variety of reasons. To some it appeared to implement a new concept of income; to others it was a step toward recognition of the "business cycle" in accounting; to the majority, probably, it has been a method of accounting accepted by the tax authorities and deemed advantageous by many taxpayers. In its more recent application it constitutes a departure from the "past cost" concept of income accounting and a form of implementation of the principle of measuring charges against revenues in units of approximately equal purchasing power.

3. The second question was: "Should accounting procedures be revised so as to bring cost of property exhaustion into account at approximately the same price level as the revenues and, if so, how should this object be accomplished?" Upon this question (to which the third is subordinate) substantial differences of opinion have existed.

4. The third question was: "Assuming social usefulness to be the objective, should the situation be met by (1) changes in methods of accounting, (2) changes in methods of presentation, or (3) supplementary information?"

5. The American and English Institutes have taken the position that the increased cost of making good the exhaustion of property owing to rise in the price levels should not be reflected in the accounts by charges in the determination of income for the year. Both have

expressed the view that such increased cost should preferably be met out of revenue. They would, however, treat this provision as made out of retained income. Thus, the Committee on Accounting Procedure of the American Institute has said:

> Stockholders, employees and the general public should be informed that a business must be able to retain out of profits amounts sufficient to replace productive facilities at current prices if it is to stay in business.[1]

6. Statistics prepared for the Group show that between 1938 and 1948 the wholesale price level rose rather more than 100 per cent, and that during the last two hundred years the value of the dollar at its highest point in any quarter-century was from 1.3 to 3 times its value at the lowest point in the same quarter-century. Manifestly, annual accounts do not attain maximum significance so long as such fluctuations are ignored in their preparation.[2]

Attitude of Accountants

7. In the discussions which have come to the attention of the Group and in its own meetings, the views expressed by accountants have varied widely. The differences have related not so much to the question of what concept of income would be most useful as to the question of how far accountants are, or should be able and willing to undertake the task of implementing a given concept.

Official Views

8. One official view of the policy underlying bulletins such as Nos. 29 and 33 was fairly summarized in the testimony of a past president of the American Institute of Accountants before the Subcommittee on Profits of the Joint Committee on the Economic Report in December, 1948:

> The American Institute of Accountants . . . has, by and large, emphasized the importance of considering income for a given year against the backdrop of the economic conditions for that year, rather than to have the impact of those economic conditions estimated, appraised individually and sporadically, in the determination of income for each company.

[1] *Accounting Research Bulletin* No. 33, *Supplementary Statement* of Oct. 14, 1948, and *Recommendation* No. XII of the English Institute.
[2] Exhibit II.

9. A second indication is a footnote in a statement of "accounting standards" issued during the same year by the American Accounting Association (representative mainly of the academic accountants) in which strict adherence to the monetary postulate was advocated:

> Readers of financial statements may be aided in their interpretations by considering the effect of fluctuations in the purchasing power of money . . . however, price changes during recent years do not afford sufficient justification for a departure from cost.

Conflicting Views

10. Those who have favored adherence to present practice have commonly talked in terms of "factual" and "objective" determinations and "uniformity." They perhaps have not given adequate recognition to the extent to which accounting is necessarily characterized by "postulates," "estimates," "subjective choice of method," and "variety in methods." [3]

11. A second group of accountants has accepted the view that the accountant has an important interpretive function which is not being discharged today as effectively as it might and should be.

12. The two groups differ in their view of the relation of the accountant toward the monetary unit, though both agree that income must be *expressed* in terms of dollars of the current year.

13. At least some of the members of the first group hold that the monetary postulate is, in the language of Veblen,

> . . . a necessary assumption in business, since business is necessarily done in terms of price; so that money values unavoidably constitute the baseline to which transactions are finally referred, and by measurements upon which they are ultimately checked, controlled, adjusted and accounted for.[4]

They take the view that financial accounts are primarily reports of stewardship and that the obligation of management is to account for the *monetary capital* invested in the corporation.

14. Upon such views members of the first group reach the conclu-

---

[3] See *Business Income and Price Levels: An Accounting Study* (published in 1949 by the Study Group), pp. 21–26.

[4] *Absentee Ownership and Business Enterprise in Recent Times* (Huebsch, 1923). p. 179.

sion that the difference between charges for exhaustion based on the cost of the property exhausted and those based on present cost of replacement should appear *outside the framework of the income account* for which the independent accountant accepts responsibility.

15. Members of the second group, taking a broader view of the character of the financial accounts, have urged that the monetary unit should be regarded as a tool to be used by the accountant with full recognition of its uses and its defects. They would have accountants take cognizance of the fact that the design of the tool is changed from time to time by its makers (Government) and that those who fashion it may seek to impart to it not stability, but a purposeful instability of purchasing power. They, therefore, believe that the efforts of accountants should be directed to presenting determinations of income in which revenue and charges against revenue would be stated as nearly as possible in units of the same purchasing power. They recognize that marked changes in the value of money create other problems which affect the balance sheet and call for consideration.

16. The members of a third group, while they did not favor taking cognizance of fluctuations in the value of the monetary unit in general, have felt that in the recent past the changes have been so great that they should be recognized through a general restatement of carrying values of the tangible assets of corporations; this they suggest would restore to the balance sheet a significance which does not now exist.

17. Some opponents of this proposal argue that its adoption would not be warranted unless (1) a similar restatement were to be made of money claims or (2) the writing up of assets were to be treated as a quasi-realization. Others have taken the position that it should not be necessary to write up book values in order to secure a proper reflection of the increased cost of exhaustion in the income statement. They have pointed out that there is no evidence of any close correlation between changes in the present value of capital assets and changes in the cost of making good exhaustion.

Attitude of the Securities and Exchange Commission

18. The Securities and Exchange Commission, in its 1949 *Annual Report,* discussing its action in regard to exhaustion charges and on the

question of accelerated depreciation (which will next be considered herein), said:

> The conclusion reached was that depreciation charges in financial statements filed with the Commission should continue to be based upon cost. Revisions of financial statements on file have been made in accordance with this conclusion. In some cases accounting recognition has been given to the high rates of production enjoyed in postwar years by accelerating depreciation charges in periods during which productive capacity was used in excess of normal average production over a representative period of years. Similarly, the amortization of plant costs incurred to capture a temporarily expanded demand was deemed to comply with the generally applicable accounting principle of matching costs with revenues. In such cases a clear explanation of the circumstances justifying the early amortization of costs has been obtained.[5]

19. The novel features of the cases to which the Commission referred were, first, the amortization of part of the cost of facilities more rapidly than the remainder, and second, increasing the amortization charge "in the early years of use when the economic usefulness of the facilities is greatest" even though this condition is due not to abnormal use of the facilities, but to abnormal demand for the product. Neither the American nor the English Institute has dealt specifically with these new procedures nor have the procedures been accepted for tax purposes or approved by the American Accounting Association.

An Accounting Proposal

20. Accountants in the second group have favored dealing with the problem within the framework of income determination by charging in respect of exhaustion, first, an amount calculated as in the past, plus or minus a separate percentage adjustment based on the relation between the current price level and the average price level on which the initial charge is computed. For the sake of convenience they would treat all property acquired prior to a basic date, such as January 1, 1940, as having been acquired at the average price level of the period preceding that date.

---

[5] *Fifteenth Annual Report of the Securities and Exchange Commission* (1949), p. 179.

21. In the discussion of this proposal by the Group, questions were raised:

    a) whether any use of a procedure of this kind was called for;

    b) whether it was possible to find or develop a suitable index;

    c) what type of index should be used, if any;

    d) whether the use of price indexes would tend to deprive a management of credit due it for wise purchasing.

Upon the first point, the facts that price indexes are now used in the application of the LIFO inventory rule for tax and general accounting purposes, and that they are used in labor-management negotiations and contracts and in other ways seem persuasive.

The Monetary Unit As the Accounting Unit

22. The defects of the medium of exchange as the standard of value for long-term indebtedness or accounting have long been recognized. Wesley C. Mitchell, our great authority on the subject, tells us that the use of index numbers began in Italy about 1785, and was developed extensively in England from about the beginning of the nineteenth century, being stimulated by price fluctuations during the Napoleonic wars. The need for a "standard of value" as distinguished from a "unit of exchange" was discussed at length in a volume published in 1833, and was thereafter given much consideration by eminent economists such as Jevons and Marshall. In 1887 Marshall lamented that there was no way to avoid speculation in the employment of capital because however safe the monetary capital might be there was an inevitable element of speculation as to its real value. He suggested the adoption of a unit of value, as distinct from the unit of currency, but derived therefrom by the use of an official price index.[6]

23. In the early days of the present century, bankers, economists, and others had come to believe that the monetary unit should and could be kept reasonably stable in purchasing power. They did not foresee the effects upon it of two world wars and forty years of social change. In 1914 a leading authority on monetary theory told a member of the Group, who thought of selecting that branch of economics as

[6] *Contemporary Review*, March, 1887. See also *Official Papers by Alfred Marshall* (London, Macmillan & Company, Ltd., 1926), p. 10.

the one on which he would concentrate, that he would be foolish to make such a choice because everything had been said on the subject that could be said.

24. In recent years monetary policy has been directed to a number of social or political objectives, such as the maintenance of full employment and low interest rates on Government debt. Stability of the monetary unit has not been a major purpose of national policy.

25. On the second point, economists who are members of the Group have pointed out that in other cases great progress had resulted from using in the first instance an admittedly imperfect index and gradually improving it. It was mentioned that a careful study by Mitchell of the cost-of-living index in wartime indicated that the defects in the indexes used were not of major importance. It was pointed out that even an imperfect index would give more significant results than ignoring changes in the value of the dollar altogether.

26. Upon the third point a major question arises whether the index to be used should be a *general* price index or a *specific* index related to the type of property disposed of or consumed.

27. The existence of the choice and the possibility that the results arrived at might vary appreciably according to the choice made are often presented as arguments against the use of any index; but the same objection could be validly urged against many of the methods of implementing accounting conventions. The differences envisioned would not be of a higher order of magnitude than those encountered in applying depreciation accounting or distributing past service costs of pensions over periods in the future (which may vary from ten to thirty years) or in many other cases.

28. Another preliminary objection may be illustrated by a quotation from the recent report of the "Tucker" committee in England. Speaking of proposals for allowing deductions from revenue in respect of property consumed or sold to be based on current price level, the Committee said:

> Before considering the various types of schemes put forward, it will be convenient to mention one objection common to all schemes, namely, that they involve giving preferential treatment to the owners of businesses as against other classes of taxpayer. The non-trader who saved a sum of

money before the war and invested it in Government securities or other fixed interest bearing securities finds that it is now worth in terms of real value a half or a third of what it was worth when he invested it, but he remains liable to tax on the full income from that and other sources; he does not get, and could not be given within the framework of the existing Income Tax system, any allowance for the loss of capital or income. The pensioner who draws his pension from a superannuation fund to which he has contributed over his working life may find that the real value of his pension is far less than the real value of the contributions that he and his employers have made.[7]

29. When the general price level rises or falls, the increases or decreases will not be uniform. It may well be that the great majority of businessmen will fare better in a period of inflation than the recipient of fixed net income. Some enterprises will be prevented by economic conditions from securing increases in their revenues as great as the increases in their costs. This might be regarded in a free enterprise system as a hazard of business and an element in the determination of profits from *activities*. But it would still be true that the source of the advantage enjoyed by the businessman was his ability to raise *revenues* and that the logical way to redress the balance would be by action on the revenue side, not on the cost or deduction side.

30. Whenever prices rise materially, there will, in practice, also be businesses which will be prevented by *governmental restriction* (either permanent or adopted to meet the situation) from increasing their revenues as much as their costs increase. Our rent-restriction laws and the whole system of regulating the revenues of utilities on the basis of monetary investment are illustrations. The generalization in the paragraph quoted is unwarranted.

31. The suggestion made in the paragraph is in effect to deny one producer a legitimate deduction because another producer may be able to more than offset a similar deduction by an increase in revenue. It can be justified only on the ground that income taxation is at best of a "hit or miss" character. No businessman should deceive himself as to his own income in any such way.

[7] *Report of the Committee on the Taxation of Trading Profits* (Feb. 20, 1951), Chap. III, Par. 100.

32. Before presenting this argument, the "Tucker" committee had reached a decision adverse to the proposals on the ground that they ran counter to the established practice of commercial accountancy and did not have the support of the accounting profession. The use of this argument emphasizes the great social responsibilities of the accountant.

33. Turning to consideration of the choice between general and specific indexes, it may be noted that in past practice LIFO accounting in the United States and the system employed by the English railways for dealing with capital assets both contemplated charges against revenues based on current price levels, and that both were implemented by the use of specific indexes appropriate to the commodities involved.

34. With respect to railways, C. H. Newton, in his book *Railway Accounts,* said:

> . . . The great increase in the cost of wages and materials arising since the war rendered such provisions [that is, charges based on the cost of property replaced] wholly inadequate for ultimate renewal of assets which were produced originally at comparatively low prices. It became necessary, therefore, in many cases to revise the basis of annual provision, and this was done by taking the estimated *renewal* cost in lieu of original capital cost.[8]

35. When the English railways were nationalized, the new authority revised the methods of accounting for equipment and certain other property by adopting the basis of depreciation on *original cost.* The result was to reduce the operating expenses for the first year by some £8 million and to create a profit of £2.8 million instead of a loss. The authority offered as one justification of this procedure the statement that, "Leading accountancy bodies in this country and the United States have recommended that depreciation provisions should be based on actual cost of the assets in use, and that any further provision towards replacement cost should be regarded as a matter of financial appropriation rather than as a process of accounting charge." [9] However, the change was characterized by the *Accountant,* the official journal of the English Institute of Accountants, as of questionable wisdom, and was severely criticized by the (London) *Economist.*

[8] (London, 1930), p. 175.
[9] *Journal of Accountancy,* July, 1951, p. 92.

36. Despite the precedents cited, it may be said that changes in prices within a stable general price level have commonly been regarded as elements in determining profits from activities. Indeed, speculation based on expectation of such changes is a recognized form of business activity. It would seem to follow that the price index to be used would preferably be one of *general purchasing power*. This point will be considered later from the economic viewpoint (*infra,* Section 6).

Purchasing Below Service Value

37. Turning to the fourth point (¶ 21), when an enterprise is acquired by a corporation through purchase or reorganization, the price paid may be greater or less than the net value of the physical assets and the monetary assets, all valued on a going-concern basis, and minus the liabilities. If the price is *greater,* the excess is treated as an intangible asset, often termed goodwill, which is usually carried indefinitely at cost, unless it is written down to a nominal figure. Where the price is *less* (the case presented when a purchase is made at less than service value), the logical procedure is to assume that the difference reflects a lack of earning capacity sufficient to support a capital equal to the net total of the going-concern values of the separate assets. It would obviously be unsound to base the subsequent accounting in respect of assets acquired in the one case on *no more than* their going-concern value and in the other on *less than* that value if in other respects the postulate of permanence were to be accepted. If the subsequent operations were to be regarded as a liquidation, the rules of accounting that are based on the postulate of "permanence" would not be applicable.

The Chicago, Great Western Railway Co. Case

38. The general view here expressed was adopted by the Interstate Commerce Commission in dealing with the problem as presented in the many railroad reorganizations since 1932, and by the Congress in respect of taxation of reorganized companies. In a decision in the case of the Chicago, Great Western Railway Co. (*Ex parte* 138), the Commission held that depreciation should be computed upon the fair service value of the property, which was much higher than the portion of the total purchase price in reorganization, which was deemed to be

allocable thereto, though the staff had advocated using the latter basis. The Commission recognized that the treatment which it adopted was called for under the prudent-investment and original-cost theories and by sound finance. The Commission said:

> It must be borne in mind that property which is carried in the accounts at a depreciated value [that is, depreciated for lack of earning power] continues in usual course to function in the operation of the railroad, and when retirement becomes necessary, it must ordinarily be replaced with new property whose cost has suffered no reduction. Gradually, therefore, as property is retired and replaced, the property investment accounts will tend to become reestablished on the basis of full original cost, and there will also be a corresponding increase in capitalization, unless the excess cost is met by appropriations of income which would otherwise be available for the payment of contingent interest or dividends.

39. Commenting on the decision, George O. May said in his *Financial Accounting*:

> In the paragraph which followed, the Commission indicated its clear understanding of the problem by distinguishing between the case of property which is replaceable and that which is retired and not replaced. It, however, decided that as a practical matter it was not possible to foresee which units of property would be abandoned, and that errors in judgment on this point might have serious financial consequences in the future. It therefore left this phase of the subject for further consideration and disposition.
>
> The practical importance of the accounting questions presented became strikingly manifest when war brought the prospect of new war taxes. It became apparent that unless the principles laid down by the Commission were implemented in the tax law, reorganizations contemplated would have to be abandoned, and that where reorganization had been consummated the tax burden on the new companies would be ruinous. The anomaly already pointed out, that lowering the book value of depreciable assets results apparently in higher earnings, would have taken an almost tragic form. A railroad which through lack of earning capacity had been forced to reorganize would have been liable to an excess profits tax from which another company which had been and still was more successful would (not having been reorganized) be free.[10]

[10] (Macmillan. 1943), pp. 114–115.

40. The Commission has not gone so far as to recognize that the logic of the prudent-investment theory requires charges for exhaustion to be based on cost of replacement rather than on the cost of what is replaced.

41. In the cases just discussed, it was the income of the enterprise as distinguished from that of the company that was carrying on the enterprise that was to be measured.

42. This discussion in turn leads to the question of how far determinations in which exhaustion charges are based on an old cost to the corporation are appropriate in a prospectus, or in annual reports made after a substantial issue of equity stock to new owners has been based on present values.

Timing of Capital Outlays

43. Consideration may next be given to cases in which purchases are advantageous by reason of timing, as, for instance, when expansion is undertaken in periods of depression and low prices. The suggested procedure of showing both depreciation on cost and a percentage adjustment would result in managements receiving due recognition in the form of a lower primary charge and a larger secondary charge for price adjustment as compared with a similar enterprise whose investment was badly timed. Expansion may be disadvantageous in respect of cost of acquisition, but advantageous because of the existence of an unusually favorable market for products of the business. It has been suggested that in such cases exhaustion charges in the early years should be above the normal. At this point the question under consideration becomes that of accelerated depreciation, which will be discussed hereinafter.

Balance-Sheet Problem

44. Accountants who have opposed recognition of changes in price level have stressed supposed difficulties in dealing in the balance sheet with the supplementary charges against revenues that have been suggested. This is not a problem of income determination, but one of accounting technique in the compilation of the balance sheet, which is complementary to the income statement in present-day accounting.

Nevertheless a brief discussion of it may throw an interesting light on concepts of business income.

45. The view expressed by the Committee on Accounting Procedure in 1938 as to the significance of the income statement (*supra,* page 19) was comparatively new. Stephen Gilman, a member of the Group, in the Preface to his *Accounting Concepts of Profit,*[11] spoke of the shift of emphasis from the balance sheet to the income statement as having taken place "in the past half dozen years." In England the Act of 1929 was the first Companies Act that made submission to stockholders of an income account compulsory.

46. When income was deemed to be the increase in net worth, it was measurable by a comparison of balance sheets; the income account merely provided a supplementary analysis which, among other things, might distinguish the income from operations from other forms of income. Today it is the balance sheet that is secondary: it is sometimes described as a statement of residuals.[12]

Answers to the Second and Third Specific Questions

47. It is difficult to see how acceptance of LIFO as now applied can long be combined with rejection of the current price level as a basis of charges for property exhaustion. The arguments in favor of the former that apply at least equally to the latter are:

a) One is as much called for by the postulate of permanence as the other.

b) Both raise the same problem on liquidation.

c) Both have the same practical merit of bringing about a closer relation between what is deemed to be income and what it is practicable to distribute.

d) Both result in an impairment of the significance of the orthodox balance sheet.

e) Both take the same view of the relation between the unit of accounting measurement and the currency unit.

[11] Ronald Press, 1939.

[12] It is a striking historical fact that the great English Companies Act of 1862 took precisely the modern view of the relation between the two statements in a model form of corporate regulations which formed an appendix to the Act and was designated Table A.

48. It would seem that if accounting is to render the full service of which it is capable, it should face the problems created by instability of the monetary unit. Accounting must follow other professions in more precise diagnoses and classifications and in more specialized treatments. This has been recognized in some branches of accounting, but financial accounting lags behind.

49. The conclusion on the whole matter is perhaps that, for the present at least, financial statements should reveal the effects of applying both the older and the newer concepts, the older concepts being implemented by the use of FIFO, or average cost, for inventories, and past cost for exhaustion charges; and the newer concept by LIFO, perhaps improved in form for inventories, and charges for exhaustion on the basis of current costs. The results of applying both concepts might or might not be revealed within the framework of the official income determinations.

Revalorization

50. The line of reasoning that has been set forth leads to the conclusion that a proposal to measure provisions for exhaustion of property in units of purchasing power would not imply, or even justify, a proposal to write up capital assets to new valuations such as was contemplated by the third group of accountants above-mentioned. As already noted, there is no evidence of any close correlation between the increase either of the monetary or of the real worth of such assets and the increase in the cost of maintaining them.

51. Taking a longer view, it might well be deemed convenient that new (or supplementary) *monetary ascriptions* should be given to these assets in order to reflect the change in the realities represented by the monetary unit. Historical cost is capable of measurement in terms of purchasing power converted into current monetary units. But this is a part of a large question of securing a better integration of the income statement with the statement of financial condition, and a better reflection of the "accountabilities" of management.

52. In the recent past write-ups have been infrequent in American industrial practice. However, mention should be made of the recent action of one of the largest of English industrial enterprises, Imperial

Chemical Industries, Ltd. That company has written up its capital assets by £96 million for the avowed purpose of securing the increased charge for property exhaustion (depreciation) which the directors deemed to be called for, and which, under English accounting practice, could be taken into the accounts after such a restatement.

53. From the standpoint of the concepts of income, it is not reasonable that whether the charge for exhaustion shall or shall not be increased shall depend on whether the directors have or have not taken such action.

54. Upon the postulate of permanence, the value of individual assets necessary to the continuance of the business is not a significant figure; their value is collective and depends on future prospects. Furthermore, if these assets had to be valued as physical assets, the measure of value might not properly be the cost of replacing them in kind, but rather the cost of the most efficient substitute, less a deduction for relative inefficiency of the existing unit and a deduction for partial exhaustion of physical life.

New Problems and Special Types of Enterprises

1. During the three years that the Group has been in existence, issues other than those raised on the three questions posed by the Executive Committee have arisen. These call for mention either because they affect the general question of concepts as vitally as, or perhaps to an even more serious extent than, the issues do which the Group expressly undertook in 1947 to consider, or because they illustrate the conflicts in objectives that are encountered in reconciling theory with practicability. Among these are:

   a) the question of accelerated depreciation, which has already been touched upon briefly;
   b) the system of lease-backs and new forms of contractual arrangements which have had an important effect on the determination of income;
   c) the problems created by new developments in the field of pensions.

Another subject on which opinions have differed is the merit of the all-inclusive income statement.

Accelerated Depreciation

2. Reference has already been made to the issue during World War II of emergency certificates under which the cost of new facilities might be charged against revenues for tax purposes over a five-year period or duration of the war, whichever might be shorter.

3. During 1948 provisions for accelerated depreciation were adopted by a relatively small number of large corporations in their own ac-

counts. These were not, however, accepted for tax purposes. The increased current charges were defended on the ground that current costs of construction were abnormally high, and that incurring them was justified only by the existence of an abnormal immediate demand. The proposals contemplated that the aggregate charges against revenue would never exceed the original cost of the plant to which they related, differing in this respect from proposals (which have already been discussed) to make charges for exhaustion of existing plant on the basis of current price levels. In testimony before the Subcommittee of the Joint Congressional Committee on the Economic Report in December of that year, acceptance of this practice for tax purposes was urged, but without success. It is perhaps for this reason that the procedure has not been more widely adopted.

4. In principle, no doubt, there is much ground for argument that reasonably foreseeable changes in profitability should be recognized as an element in the allocation of depreciation charges between years, since the object of creating facilities is to secure profits. In the past a controlling objection to acceptance of the proposal has been the subjective and unverifiable nature of the assumptions that would be necessary.

5. The problem illustrates the conflict between the desire for significance and the demand for objectivity which is constantly presented in accountancy.

6. It is significant that the Securities and Exchange Commission has accepted statements in which such charges were made upon condition of full disclosure of the treatment and its effect. Thus, the development seems to point the way to the answer to other questions which the Group has been considering; namely, that changes in practice should take the form, at least in the first instance, of more effective disclosure rather than an attempt to evolve a new unique measurement of income to govern companies in general or any particular class of companies.

Lease-backs

7. There has developed a practice of selling commercial plants to insurance companies, or others, with a concurrent lease to the vendor

on bases that go far to ensure the return of the purchaser's investment with a larger rate of yield than insurance companies can ordinarily secure. In some cases the effect has been merely to substitute leasehold obligations for capital obligations. In other cases, by varying the rentals from year to year, it has been possible also for the manufacturer-vendor-lessee to secure in his own accounts, if not also for tax purposes, current deductions for rent as large as interest on the sales price and depreciation on replacement cost combined. The following quotation from an annual report of 1949 illustrates the procedure in an extreme form:

> During the year the construction of a plant at —— was completed at a total cost of $1,159,300. This plant was sold to an insurance company at cost and a subsidiary leased the property for a period of five years at an annual rental of $262,587 plus the cost of taxes, maintenance and protection. The subsidiary has the right to renew the lease for periods totalling forty-five years at an annual rental of $11,593 plus the cost of taxes, maintenance and protection.

8. In such cases of this type, the lessor no doubt, being normally a financial enterprise, will determine its income each year on the basis of the annual yield over the term of the lease, assuming that any options to the lessee will be exercised in the manner least favorable to the lessor.

9. To the lessee the lease-back, if made in good faith, reflects the view that the capital investment is made largely with a short-run object in view, and that the income from it may be most fairly reflected by charging the stipulated rental against current revenue. In some cases, as for instance those of textile enterprises which had a long record of unsuccessful operation but were acquired in the expectation of a few postwar years of high profits, such an approach may be regarded as being a realistic, even though subjective, recognition of probabilities. However, such enterprises should perhaps be treated as among those to which the postulate of permanence is not properly applicable.

10. The research bulletin dealing with lease-backs (*Accounting Research Bulletin* No. 38) is entitled, "Disclosure of Long-Term Leases in Financial Statements of Lessees," and the Securities and Exchange

Commission has also dealt with the problem as mainly one of disclosure.

11. Whether the lease-back will become a permanent and important feature of corporate financing may depend largely on the treatment finally accorded to such transactions for income tax and other purposes. However, it is significant for the present purpose if only as an illustration of the tendency to create artificial contractual relations for the purpose of affecting determinations of income for tax or other purposes.

Pensions

12. The pension problem may be of greater importance than those that have been considered up to now. The crux of it, from the accounting standpoint, is the treatment of what is called the "past service liability," that is, the portion of the future pension payment which will become payable because of services rendered prior to the initiation of the pension plan.

13. The magnitude of the problem is indicated by the fact that in the case of the United States Steel Corporation the present value of this liability was estimated actuarially at about $574 million, which is about 50 per cent of the market value of the preferred and common stock of the corporation at the time when the contract was entered into.

14. The assumption of an obligation of this kind and magnitude— to pay A a pension, although he may retire under the plan the day after the plan is adopted, in order to secure the labor of others in the future—may be regarded from different viewpoints.

15. In one view it may be regarded by the payor as well as the payee as additional compensation for services in the past. From this point of view, upon the all-inclusive concept of income the charge against income of the year of the present value of the liability at the time when the liability is incurred might be considered necessary. Such a view would be more theoretical than practical.

16. At the other extreme there is the view that upon the postulate of permanence the obligation might be dealt with simply in a footnote. This proposal may seem startling, but if accounting ignores the great shrinkage in the value of assets that would result if the enterprise were

abandoned, it may be asked why should it make a double charge against revenues for pensions over a period of years, first for those currently accruing, and second, for those rooted in the past, seeing that the reserve created for the second charge will assume practical importance only in the event of abandonment.

17. Still another view might take into account the possibilities that an initial demand once granted will lead to still greater demands in the future with retroactive effects, or that public policy will call for the whole problem to be dealt with by Government and financed by taxation.

18. The middle course of spreading the past service charges over a period of years in the future accompanied by full disclosure seems to be a practical and acceptable solution. If *income from operations* is to be determined, perhaps the charge in respect of past service (less the relative tax reduction) might be regarded as coming after the determination of operating income.

19. If the charge is to be distributed over the future, it is not possible to select a period in the future over which it should logically be distributed. In practice the procedure has been determined largely by the fact that for tax purposes the deduction may be spread over a period of not less than ten years; probably the greater part of the liability is being charged over that minimum period.

20. In its one bulletin on the subject, *Accounting Research Bulletin* No. 36, November, 1948, the Committee on Accounting Procedure reached unanimously the negative conclusion that "costs of annuities based on past services should not be charged to surplus," and the positive conclusion that "costs of annuities based on past services should be allocated to current and future periods; provided, however, that if they are not sufficiently material in amount to distort the results of operations in a single period, they may be absorbed in the current year."

The All-Inclusive Concept of Income

21. Differences of opinion have arisen on a specific question involving the concept of business income: whether one figure should be singled out for emphasis as "net income for the year" and, if so, upon what

view of income for the year that figure should be determined. Some have favored what is called the all-inclusive concept, according to which income for the year is total income since an initial date, less income already attributed to earlier years. Others have emphasized the income that results from operations of the year. (Both groups would in practice absorb in the computation for the year minor items which are the inevitable corrections of past determinations.)

22. The controversy may seem a technical one, but its existence, its origin, and the nature of the contentions throw light on the general subject which the Group is considering.

23. In an earlier day it was the accepted view that the computation of income for the year was at best a "matter of estimate and opinion," to use the words of Lord Justice Buckley (Lord Wrenbury), and it was regarded as prudent to carry a reserve or surplus, against which might be charged costs arising out of past events which might later come to light. The right to make direct charges against this surplus was frequently abused; indeed, a more objectionable practice also developed of charging items against surplus created out of capital.

24. In the report to the Stock Exchange in 1932 (mentioned above), the Institute's Committee recommended that this latter practice should be banned; the Institute adopted this proposal. The Institute has also repeatedly urged strict limitation of the practice of making charges to surplus. But it has pointed out that inclusion in the income statement of all costs and charges arising out of past operation would at times, even though it may be seldom, make the income reported a meaningless or misleading figure. Nevertheless, there have been many who have favored absolute prohibition of charges to surplus, though most of them perhaps have also favored inclusion of extraordinary charges in a separate division of the income statement.

25. Essentially the controversy is the result of the unwarranted importance that has become attached to a figure described as "net income for the year" as a result of its use in statistical services and elsewhere. Both parties agree that the figure is not entitled to the weight accorded it, and that full disclosure and due consideration of extraordinary items are essential to an intelligent conclusion as to the results of corporate

operations, but each party naturally seeks to establish its right to the use of the particular phrase.[1] Probably neither should use it without amplification.

The Relation Between Financial- and Tax-Accounting

26. In general, it is desirable that financial-accounting and tax-accounting should be as nearly the same as possible. This is recognized in tax laws of both the United States and Great Britain, nevertheless, in practice differences are unavoidable.

27. If, with taxes at high levels, charges affect the tax burden in one year but are brought into financial accounts in another, the significance of the accounts is lessened. However, the fact that the Congress denies the right to deduct a charge in determining taxable income of a year does not, in itself, warrant exclusion of the charge from the financial accounts, and a deduction permitted by the Congress may be in the nature of a relief of a part of income from taxation rather than a necessary charge in measuring income for general corporate purposes.

28. The Congress might perhaps have exercised even more influence than it has on the development of concepts of income if it had undertaken to distinguish clearly between these two types of deductions. Manifestly political considerations often dictated the opposite course.

29. Enactments relating to the use of the LIFO method of inventorying and deductions in respect of pension plans, two instances of major importance already discussed, have greatly affected methods of income determination adopted in business practice.

30. More broadly, when income taxes approach or exceed 50 per cent, the existence of the tax and the way in which it is measured cannot be ignored in deciding between methods of financial-accounting.

Capital Gains and Business Income

31. The insistence of the courts on realization as necessary to the recognition of income under the Sixteenth Amendment has already been discussed. A departure from this principle, particularly in relation to the taxation of capital gains of *individuals,* has been strongly advo-

[1] Cf. *Accounting Research Bulletin* No. 32.

cated by some; that subject does not come within the scope of the study undertaken in this report.

32. If capital gains of business corporations realized, or unrealized, are to be treated as income, they clearly constitute a special category of income which should be sharply distinguished from the income derived from purchase or manufacture and sale of goods and services in the ordinary course of business.

33. This view has been generally accepted; segregation in statements to be submitted to the Securities and Exchange Commission is made mandatory by the Investment Companies Act of 1940 in the case of financial and investment companies in which such capital gains assume special importance.

34. As long as the accounting of a commercial corporation is conducted on the assumption of permanence, fluctuations in the value of separate assets necessary to the conduct of the business have little relevance. If any such assets are sold otherwise than in a liquidation of the business, or of a major component thereof, the proceeds will in the natural course of accounting enter into the determination of the final aggregate charges for property exhaustion. When liquidations occur, new rules become applicable.

35. Often, as in the case of gas stations or "taxpayer" buildings, an expected appreciation in value of land is an element in the decision to make the investment. In such cases a capital gain may ultimately be realized that may be regarded as a form of business income. Here again, disclosure and effective presentation seem to be indicated as the proper treatment.

Special Types of Enterprises

36. So far consideration has been given only to the typically large corporation whose securities are listed and which has adopted the postulate of permanence. We have found that there is for them no unique concept of business income that will serve all purposes adequately, and that what is needed at the present time is information that will facilitate the determination of income according to more than one concept.

Small Private Corporations

37. As Edward B. Wilcox and Howard C. Greer in their report to the Study Group pointed out:

> Accounts are kept, profits are computed, and policy decisions are made by several hundred thousand individual businessmen and their bookkeepers and clerks. Most of them would have grave difficulty in applying or even comprehending the principles of measuring cost expirations in terms of hypothetical purchasing power. The economic data available to them are certain to be inadequate and their interpretations of several dozen tables of price-index numbers are likely to be diverse to say the least. Depreciation calculations contain enough elements of variation now; price-index adjustments would so magnify the inconsistencies as to render the computations meaningless.[2]

The authors of the report anticipated that their language might be regarded as "defeatist," but the real point is that it does not apply to large publicly owned corporations and therefore its significance, from either the financial or social point of view, is very limited.

38. There is no public interest which calls for applying to the hundreds of thousands of small corporations, whose management and ownership are closely combined, requirements deemed appropriate for the guidance of investors in the few thousand large corporations whose securities are widely distributed. They should, of course, be free to adopt them. Nor should the requirements to be exacted from the listed corporations be measured by the needs of the owners or the competence of the bookkeepers of small private ventures. The owners of these small ventures will have ready to hand the information necessary to implement any concept of income that may be significant to them for a particular purpose; this is not true of the small investor in the larger corporation. The service which accounting renders to this type of enterprise, though important, is of a character different from that rendered to the large company whose ownership is widely distributed.

The difference between types of corporations is obscured in our system by the existence of forty-eight states in which a business may

[2] *Ill. Cert. Acc.,* Sept., 1950.

be incorporated. In Great Britain a distinction is made between "public" and "private" companies. In 1944 there were 13,900 of the former and 169,200 of the latter.

Financial Corporations

39. Financial corporations constitute another class to be considered. They have no inventory problem and only relatively insignificant problems in relation to wasting physical assets; their assets and liabilities are nearly all in the nature of money claims. Fluctuations in the value of the monetary unit create no problems in their determination of income from domestic operations. They do, no doubt, affect the real value of that income, but only as all income is affected.

40. A proposal to measure income in real rather than monetary terms can hardly be considered as within the realms of the practical. As has been pointed out, such a proposal is neither made nor implicit in the suggestion that the positive and negative elements in determining monetary income should be expressed in units of the same purchasing power.

Limited-Term Enterprises

41. Another class of cases not yet considered comprises corporations engaged in single ventures or in operations the continuance of which is subject to a natural limitation which makes the postulate of permanence, or indefinite life, inapplicable. This class includes corporations owning business or residential buildings, some engaged in the extractive industries (though many of these adopt the postulate of permanence), single-ship companies, and a great variety of small business ventures. Such corporations form a relatively insignificant proportion of those whose securities are held by the general public. Broadly, it may be said that each class presents a special problem, and that these cases have relatively little significance in relation to the subject of concepts of income. Their treatment may be regarded as problems for accountants.

Economic Considerations

1. The two aspects of the problem under examination with which economists are most concerned are the broad concept of income to be selected and the role of money. The first has been discussed in Section 2; the second is crucial in relation to the specific problems selected for special examination by the Group. In discussing it we shall rely mainly on a memorandum prepared by Solomon Fabricant.

2. In two remarkable essays on the role of money in economic development, Wesley Mitchell drew attention to "the many ways in which the use of money has influenced the fortunes of successive generations. . . ." The use of money is one of "the great rationalizing habits" of behavior slowly evolved by society. "It gives society the technical machinery of exchange, the opportunity to combine personal freedom with orderly cooperation on a grand scale, and the basis of that system of accountancy which Sombart appropriately calls 'economic rationalism.' " [1] The introduction of money into the dealings of men thus enlarged their economic and political freedom, increased their efficiency, accelerated improvements in the methods of producing and distributing goods and in the development of new products and led to the reorganization of society.

3. But, Mitchell emphasized, the use of money brought with it "trouble as well as gain." "It exposed a nation to a novel set of dangers arising from the technical exigencies of monetary systems," for example, the host of problems connected with the use of paper money. "These technical problems were urgent because in a money economy livelihood

---

[1] "The Role of Money in Economic Theory," *American Economic Review*, Supplement, VI (March, 1916) (reprinted in *The Backward Art of Spending Money* [1937], pp. 149–176); "The Role of Money in Economic History," *The Tasks of Economic History*, a supplemental issue of the *Journal of Economic History*, Dec., 1944, pp. 61–67. Quotations are from both these papers.

itself depends upon the orderly functioning of an intricate system of production and distribution, which in turn depends upon price margins, and prices are affected in bewildering ways by money." Nor have we yet "fully mastered the monetary systems we set up. They still do unexpected and unpleasant things to us."

4. "Unpleasant" is certainly one way to characterize what inflation is doing to us today. The current discussion of the concept and measurement of business income marks the appearance of one of "the host of problems" that the operation of a money economy throws up. Mitchell's insight into the role of money in economic life should heighten our awareness of the danger that confronts us.

5. His teaching should also deepen our appreciation of the difficulties that stand in the way of meeting this danger. For one reason why money does unpleasant things to us is that its use conditions "the minds of the generations that have developed that 'great rationalizing habit.' Our minds become obsessed by monetary illusions." The use of money molds not only man's objective behavior, it also becomes "part of his subjective life, giving him a method and an instrument for the difficult task of assessing the relative importance of dissimilar goods in varying quantities, and affecting the interests in terms of which he makes his valuations." Through long practice and custom, we come to believe that money provides an infallible measure of value. Our legal, business, and accounting practices and institutions come to reflect this belief. And this creates our present problem, which may be put thus: Accounting habits that were adapted to, and proved their great usefulness in one set of circumstances threaten, by their very force as habits, to undo us in another set of circumstances to which they are ill-adapted.

6. In Section 3 emphasis is laid on the fact that accounting rests "on a framework of postulates and assumptions which are accepted and acceptable as being useful. . . ." [2] We may appreciate the point if we stop to consider that it is not peculiar to accounting. All procedures rest on a framework of assumptions or fictions. Every science is full of them. Their worth depends, as is said of accounting postulates, on their usefulness, not on their "truth." Indeed, many scientific assumptions—for example, that light is a wave—are avowedly fictions, accepted because

[2] "Business Income," *Accountant* (Vol. CXXIII), Sept. 30, 1950.

they yield satisfactory results in particular sets of circumstances. When they do not, they are replaced by other assumptions that do yield such results, for example, that light is a particle. We must always be aware, therefore, that assumptions are to be justified by their utility. Their usefulness is "always open to reconsideration." The history of scientific progress is a history of outworn fictions and assumptions, useful in their time and place, not useful in some other time and place.

7. The fundamental fictions or postulates of accounting are listed in Section 3 as the "realization postulate," the "monetary postulate," and the "postulate of permanence." Here we are concerned only with the "monetary postulate," "that fluctuations in value of the monetary unit may properly be ignored." [3]

8. It would be possible to define income in terms of money, to say, as is sometimes said, that income is a purely money concept. Unless we are prepared to do this, we have only a postulate that is obviously a fiction; changes are never absent. Yet it is obviously a useful postulate when such changes are either mere short-time fluctuations or, if consistent in directions, are relatively small. Its usefulness lies in the fact that some other (competing) assumption, though it would yield a better result, would complicate accounting calculations and increase their cost without yielding a *sufficiently* better result.

9. The goodness of an accounting result is to be measured by the consequences that ensue upon accepting it and acting accordingly. When changes in the value of money are small, the consequences flowing from acceptance of the monetary postulate cannot be much different from those that would follow upon the acceptance of a "better" postulate. However, when circumstances change and changes in the value of money become large, such differences in consequences may be substantial. The cost and trouble of an alternative, less convenient postulate may therefore be warranted.

10. With what consequences need we concern ourselves? These depend, of course, on the purposes to which accounts are put. Whether the consequences are better or worse depends, in part, on the point of view. Let us consider two major purposes of accounts: (1) to assist in guiding

---

[3] It should be remembered, however, that the several postulates in fact form a complementary set. Therefore, the usefulness of no one of them can adequately be considered apart from that of the others.

investment decisions; (2) to assist in the division of the income originating in business among the several claimants. Let us take as our point of view that of society at large. Let us compare the consequences flowing from the acceptance of the monetary postulate with those that would flow from the acceptance of an alternative postulate, which we may call the "purchasing power postulate." It is the assumption that some specified general index of prices portrays (inversely) the course of the value of money.[4] It is clear that the "purchasing power postulate," like the monetary postulate, is a fiction. It is not "true." Yet this is no criticism of it. The acid test is, as always, its usefulness.

11. The factors that determine investment decisions are being very widely discussed by economists. Though there is little agreement on the full theory, most economists would allot some weight to calculated business income, current and past, as a factor operating directly or indirectly on current investment decisions. This measure of agreement is sufficient for our purpose. We may say, then, that investment decisions—one purpose we have selected—are guided in part by accounts. Since accounts are always based on postulates that are fictions, investment decisions are in some degree imperfect, misguided. This means, from a social point of view, two things: there is always some misallocation of available investment resources among alternative uses; and there is always more or less than the optimum amount of investment.[5] When the value of money is subject to small changes, with little net drift in any direction, the monetary postulate basic to business accounts can have little distorting effect on the investment decisions guided by

---

[4] No attempt is made to specify the index, beyond stating that it ought to be based on the prices of a wide variety of goods and services, reasonably weighted. For the present purpose we might accept the cost-of-living index, an index like Snyder's, or the Bureau of Labor Statistics wholesale price index. Had time permitted, it would have been desirable to consider the more elaborate alternative of a variety of indexes, each purporting to measure (inversely) the value of money in or to a particular sector of the economy. It is assumed, of course, that the "purchasing power postulate" is utilized in an effective way in calculating business income. Its use could mean (1) simply the LIFO treatment of inventories and the replacement-cost type of adjustment of depreciation charges, or (2) the expression of all calculations in terms of units of a constant purchasing power. The economist would advocate the latter; but we need not quarrel about this choice here. (See Comments by Clark Warburton, p. 128.)

[5] It is curious, however, that J. M. Keynes himself thought that the difficulties involved in defining net income, net capital formation, and the general price level are merely "conundrums," " 'purely theoretical' in the sense that they never perplex, or indeed enter in any way into, business decisions and have no relevance to the causal sequence of economic events" (*The General Theory of Employment, Interest and Money* [London, Macmillan, 1936], p. 39; but cf. his later discussion, pp. 58 *et seq.*).

the accounts. When the value of money is subject to large changes, or even small changes that persistently drift in a single direction, the effects may be greater. Let us consider only the case of an upward trend in the price level.[6]

12. Fabricant has pointed out[7] that the impact of inflation may be greater on the business accounts of one industry than on those of another. The factors involved are (1) variation, among industries, in the importance of physical assets, (2) variation in the rate of turnover of physical assets, (3) variation in the average age—or year of acquisition—of capital assets, (4) variation in the rate of rise in prices paid for physical assets, and (5) variation in the accounting procedures followed. If the "monetary postulate" is assumed, all five sources of variation are present. If the "purchasing power postulate" is assumed, there are (substantially) only the fourth and fifth. To the extent that the calculated business income of an industry influences investment in it, there is likelihood of greater misallocation of investment resources among industries on the monetary than on the purchasing power postulate. On the monetary postulate there will presumably tend to be excessive investment, compared with the quantities on the purchasing power postulate, in industries in which physical assets are more important, older, and less frequently turned over, and deficient investment in industries of the opposite type. It is not easy to be precise, for we cannot really abstract (as we are doing) from the other effects of understatement of depreciation charges and cost of materials drawn from inventory that result from the monetary postulate. But our main point stands: misallocation is likely to be worse on the monetary than on the purchasing power postulate.

13. It seems probable that, with aggregate business income substantially overstated on the monetary postulate, and only slightly over- or understated on the purchasing power postulate, total business investment will tend to be larger in the former than in the latter case. That is, investment will be excessively stimulated.

---

[6] The case of cyclical fluctuations in prices is interesting but cannot be discussed here. In this connection, F. Schmidt's "Die Industriekonjunktur—ein Rechenfehler" (*Zeitschrift für Betriebswirtschaft*, 2. Sonderheft, Berlin, 1927) is relevant.

[7] "The Varied Impact of Inflation on the Calculation of Business Income," reprinted in *Five Monographs on Business Income*, July 1, 1950, pp. 155–159.

Business accounts play a part also in the division of the income produced in an industry among suppliers of capital, management, labor, and government. In such instances business income taxes will tend to be higher on the monetary than on the purchasing power postulate. It is likely also that wages will tend to be higher: textbooks on collective bargaining include "ability to pay" among the factors determining wages. And salaries, pension contributions, and bonuses to management may also tend to be higher. It is hard to understand fully the trends of the past twenty years in the distribution of national income without reference to these effects of current accounting practices. Presumably, too, these effects have been more serious in those industries in which physical assets are of above-average importance and age, and of below-average frequency of turnover.

14. Not all businessmen and investors are naïve readers of the accounts put into their hands. The use of LIFO, of accelerated depreciation, of supermaintenance charges, of leasing arrangements, and of high rates of corporate savings, indicates that adjustments are frequently made to the strict monetary postulate. It might be argued, therefore, that the consequences of the monetary postulate are not quite as serious as they might seem; but that is hardly an argument against the explicit and uniform replacement of a postulate which is having detrimental effects by a postulate that is more useful. Use of the purchasing power postulate in business accounting would put into the hands of those already aware of the problem a better set of figures than they can make up themselves from accounts based on the monetary postulate. It should awaken those as yet unaware of the problem and provide them also with the information they need.

15. Economists concerned with national income over long periods of years would naturally welcome statistics of corporate income expressed in the dollars of the year for which computed; they could apply price indexes where necessary for comparative purposes.

Tax Economics

16. In discussions of the Group, economists interested in problems of income taxation have laid stress on the argument that any business

which escapes the loss or disadvantage resulting from the reduction in purchasing power of the monetary unit that is suffered generally by owners of fixed incomes as a result of inflation receives a benefit or gain that is relative only, but is analogous to certain types of gain which enter into the determination of taxable income. With rates of taxation high, this is a point of major importance.

17. This point has been touched upon in Section 4, Paragraph 28 *et seq*. It has there been pointed out that the advantage does not exist where business revenues are restricted to what is held to be a fair return on monetary investment; that the extent of the advantage depends on the extent of the ability to raise prices and should therefore logically be dealt with on the revenue side; and that there is no close correlation between the extent of the advantage and the rise in costs of making good exhaustion so that it cannot be dealt with on the cost side with any approach to equity.

18. The problem is one of the incidence of inflation, and in considering it inflation may be regarded as a burden resulting from governmental policy which should fall as nearly equitably as possible.

19. We may first compare the position of a holder of an E Bond and a public utility regulated on the basis of "original cost" and "prudent investment." The E bondholder who paid $75 for it ten years ago receives $100 which has the purchasing power that $60 had when he bought it. He has income of $25 and suffers an "inflation" burden of $40.

20. The utility suffers an exactly similar burden when its compensation for *use* of its facilities is based on its investment in *old* dollars and paid in *current* dollars.

21. If its compensation for *exhaustion* is also based on the investment in *old* dollars but paid in *current* dollars and insufficient to make good the exhaustion, the utility suffers an additional inflation burden.

22. This seems clear; the issue is, however, sometimes confused by introducing the question of increased efficiency in replacement. But that consideration bears only on the quantum, not on the evaluation of the exhaustion. It is irrelevant to the issue whether the charge should be a given number of dollars or that number adjusted by a price index.

The Theory of Regulation

23. The general theory of regulation of utilities, under which the original-cost concept was evolved, is that they should be allowed the opportunity to earn revenues necessary to attract capital into the industry which implies that costs should be made good and a fair return on investment be yielded. And if it is conceded that the full cost of replacement should be met out of revenue, it is obviously preferable that it should be allowed as a cost rather than as additional income above that needed for distribution to security holders and for reserve. If we assume replacement cost to be 75 per cent above "original cost" and income tax to be 40 per cent, it is apparent that an extra dollar allowed as income will yield only $0.60 toward the excess cost of replacement, so that for every dollar of depreciation on original cost it will be necessary to allow $1.25 of income, which, after deduction of tax, will leave the $0.75 that would suffice if the allowance was made as a cost and not subject to tax.

24. If, then, the general theory is to be implemented in fact, the treatment of increased cost of replacement as a necessary *appropriation* of income increases the cost of service to the consumer and is itself inflationary. It is doubtless true that at least up to a very recent date utility managements showed no disposition to advocate the treatment of the excess of replacement cost over depreciation on original cost as a necessary provision out of revenues either before or after arriving at a figure described as income. But the obvious explanation is that, unless the charge is recognized in rates of charges permitted or for tax purposes, the effect of such recognition would be to reduce reported available income. This would make more difficult and expensive the raising of new capital to defray costs that should be financed as costs of operation.

25. The question of "efficiency," though not relevant to the immediate issue under discusion, is itself important in relation to concepts of income. If we accept the postulate of permanence and the assumption of a progressive economy, then there should in principle be charged against revenue the cost of maintaining the facilities of the enterprise in a state of efficiency, relative to that of other enterprises with which it is in direct or indirect competition, as high as the instal-

lation had when first put into service. Upon this point Sanders, Hatfield, and Moore said,

> Broadly speaking, a plant should be maintained out of revenue in a state of efficiency corresponding to the normal progress of the manufacturing arts in that industry.[8]

The criterion is not a precise one, but few accounting criteria are.

Unregulated Industries

26. We turn from the utilities to the unregulated heavy industries. They would not escape the general inflation burden merely because they were allowed exhaustion charges based on current price levels for tax purposes. How far they would do so would depend on the extent to which their sales prices are determined by fixing profit margins, or the margins by prices; in general practice there is an interaction between the two. This point has already been discussed in Section 4 (*supra*, page 55). There is little to suggest that profits of the steel industry (to take an important illustration) have in recent years been more than a reasonable return on the monetary investment, though they have no doubt been large in comparison with the meager profits of the 1930's.[9]

27. From the over-all point of view, there may be a substantial offset to the undercharges for exhaustion caused by basing depreciation on low past costs in the form of accelerated amortization of current high costs under emergency certificates or otherwise (*supra*, page 45).

28. Some contend that an adjustment of current charges is insufficient, and that present and future revenue should bear a charge in respect of inadequacy of the unexpended portion of *past* provisions for exhaustion to meet the *present* cost of making good that exhaustion. It may fairly be argued, however, that there is no good reason why money claims in which such an unexpended provision is invested should receive preferential treatment and escape the "inflation burden" that falls on other investments in money claims.

29. Unquestioning acceptance of the monetary postulate is some-

---

[8] T. H. Sanders, H. R. Hatfield, U. Moore, *A Statement of Accounting Principles* (American Institute of Accountants, 1938), p. 35.

[9] Cf. Ralph C. Jones, "The Effect of Inflation on Capital and Profits: The Record of Nine Steel Companies," *Journal of Accountancy*, Jan., 1949.

times defended on the ground that "income is a money concept." But today it can hardly be said wages are *conceived* in terms of money even though they are finally *expressed* in money. In wage negotiations it is recognized by both sides that money is a medium, a symbol, and that the real question is what a given amount of money wages will buy.

Forces in Opposition

30. The obstacles that stand in the way of acceptance of the idea of taking cognizance of changes in the purchasing power of the dollar in measuring charges for exhaustion of property are obvious. It is much simpler for the average person to close his eyes to the facts and act as if the dollar still meant what it used to mean. It is easy also to say that everyone has to accept the risk of change in the value of the currency unit and to ignore the varying effects of the change on different parties. The pressure to do so is great.

31. The Government under which inflation has taken place is apt to think that the less said about the change, the better. It may even "point with pride" to the increase in gross national product even when that represents no increase in production, but only an upward movement in the price level.

32. The financial entities which do business in money claims have virtually no problem of exhaustion of physical capital; their assets and liabilities, their revenues and costs move automatically from one level of purchasing power to another.

33. The industries which are maintained by current expenditures for intangibles (advertising, research, and so forth) immediately charged off suffer no understatement of costs and make no overstatement of income; their revenues and costs are in the same dollars.

34. The light industries, if they employ LIFO inventory accounting, are adversely affected only in respect of physical capital, and to a very limited extent.

35. Labor refuses to ignore changes in price levels, and is quick to demand and secure increases in wages for its current services commensurate with the changes in price levels of commodities. Its direct interest in past investment is relatively small.

36. The heavy industries, which employ large amounts of consumable

capital assets, that have a fairly long life, suffer the heavy burden; the extent is greater according as more of the exhaustion goes through depreciation accounts rather than maintenance accounts, and according to the extent that there are offsets in the form of extraordinary amortization of emergency facilities or "accelerated" depreciation.

37. Existing differences in methods are strikingly illustrated by the fact that in the case of the railroads 70 per cent or more of exhaustion charges go through maintenance on the basis of current costs, whereas in the case of electric utilities 70 per cent go through depreciation accounts on the basis of costs of past years.[10]

Technical Problems

38. The LIFO method is not an entirely satisfactory method of achieving an approach to the economist's objective, though its defects for this purpose are lessened when adjustments are based on price indexes. What he is interested in is that current costs shall be expressed, as nearly as may be, in terms of current dollars, and that "income" imputed to revaluation of inventories and fixed assets be excluded. The technical methods of accomplishing this are the responsibility of the accountants. The resourcefulness they have displayed in solving other problems encourages the hope that they will prove equal to the needs of the economists. If they decline the task, the adjustments which the economists will have to make in measuring the income of the nation, or of an industry, will be *unnecessarily* rough estimates. Failure to make such adjustments leads to errors which become increasingly serious as changes in price levels become greater.

39. The simple underlying concept is that business is moving from one monetary plane to another while it is being conducted.

[10] *Business Income and Price Levels: An Accounting Study*, p. 38.

SECTION 7

Legal Considerations

1. The law's concern in the determination of income is largely indirect. Whether and in what circumstances a portion of the wealth held by or coming into the ownership of any person should be classed as income as distinguished from capital are of concern to the law only as they affect the rights and duties of such person to other persons or to the State. Where taxes payable to the State are measured by income,—where to protect creditors corporations are prohibited from paying dividends out of capital,—where a corporation agrees to give certain employees a share in its profits,—where the price which a public utility company is permitted to charge consumers is to be fixed so as to yield a fair return on the company's investment,—where one party makes representations to another with respect to its capital and income,—where it is necessary to make a determination of income and principal as between a life tenant and the remainderman,—where it is necessary to determine what expenditures are properly chargeable to income and what are properly charged as capital expenditures in determining the amount of income available to the holders of income debentures or to the holders of preferred stock, dividends on which are accumulated only to the extent earned,—in these and other like situations the law may be called upon to explain or to construe what the particular parties involved had in mind when they referred to "income."

2. Because in these cases the law's primary function is to see that justice is done between the parties, the courts when asked to determine what is meant by income must, in each case, consider the term "income" in the context in which it is employed. In the case of a statute they must consider the purpose for which the statute was enacted. In the case of a contract they must consider the intent of the particular parties. Consequently, the pronouncements of the law, whether set forth in statutes or

84

in court decisions, on the subject of income may vary considerably between one case and another; yet these variations are as to borderline points; for common to all its pronouncements on this subject is the basic concept that income is something distinct from capital.[1]

Taxation

3. The practice of requiring subjects to contribute a certain portion of their income, as distinct from capital, to the sovereign goes back to ancient times, when in an agricultural society the farmer would pay taxes out of his annual harvest. Land taxes in England were, traditionally, based on the annual return of the property. The excise taxes and customs duties which traders and merchants were required to pay were intended in practice to come out of income. The direct taxation of merchants and traders measured by their incomes was introduced in England for the first time during the Napoleonic Wars, such income tax being first imposed in 1799, repealed in 1802, reenacted in 1803, and with the end of war repealed again in 1816. For the next quarter of a century there was no income tax. Then, in 1842, when England adopted its free-trade policy, the income tax was reintroduced to provide the revenue which had formerly been obtained from customs duties.

4. While there has been no precise definition of income under the English income tax law, it may be said generally that such law long regarded income as consisting of items of receipt or profit of a recurring nature. For example, the Income Tax Act of 1918 of the United Kingdom, the basis of England's present income tax system, speaks of "The annual profits or gains arising or accruing—(i) to any person residing in the United Kingdom from any kind of property whatever . . . and (ii) . . . from any trade, profession, employment, or vocation. . . ." As a result of the report of the Royal Commission on income taxation of 1920, the concept was extended to include gains from isolated transactions of an essentially trading character.

---

[1] Sometimes by statute there is delegated to an administrative body, such as the Interstate Commerce Commission, authority to prescribe systems of accounts for particular businesses subject to their supervision. In such cases the courts have frequently held that the administrative body may exercise its judgment on borderline points in distinguishing capital from income, and the courts are reluctant to disturb the administrative body's determination unless it is so arbitrary as to be an expression of a whim rather than an exercise of judgment. *Kansas City Southern Rrailroad Company* v. *United States,* 231 U.S. 423, 447 (1913); *United States* v. *New York Telephone Company,* 256 U.S. 638, 655 (1946).

5. In the United States, although an income tax was imposed by the Federal Government for a few years during and immediately following the Civil War, and again for a few years following the panic of 1893, the basis for the Federal income tax today is the Sixteenth Amendment to the United States Constitution, which was proposed on July 31, 1909, and became operative, after ratification by the legislatures of thirty-six states, on February 25, 1913. The Amendment is of great importance because otherwise the United States Constitution forbids any direct Federal tax on the ownership of wealth or the fruits of wealth of an individual, without apportionment among the several states. The Sixteenth Amendment provides:

> The Congress shall have power to lay and collect taxes on incomes, from whatever source derived, without apportionment among the several States, and without regard to any census or enumeration.

There is no definition of the word "incomes" or "income" in the Constitution or in any of the Amendments to the Constitution; and the courts have been called upon to construe what the Sixteenth Amendment meant.

6. The United States Supreme Court has said:

> Income within the meaning of the Sixteenth Amendment is the fruit that is born of capital. . . . With few exceptions, if any, it is income as the word is known in the common speech of man.[2]

Reference to the ordinary meaning of the word "income" in common speech in interpreting the Sixteenth Amendment is based on the theory that such meaning was what the State legislatures had in mind when they ratified the Amendment.[3]

7. In passing upon what is the ordinary meaning of the term "income" the courts have said:

> Income may be defined as gain derived from capital, from labor, or from both combined, including profit gained through the sale or conversion of capital.[4]

[2] *U. S.* v. *Safety Car Heating & Lighting Co.,* 297 U.S. 88, 99 (1936).
[3] *Union Trust Co. of Pittsburgh* v. *Commissioner of Internal Revenue,* CCA—3, 115 F. (2d) 86 (1940), certiorari denied, 312 U.S. 700 (1941).
[4] *Bowers* v. *Kerbaugh-Empire Co.,* 271 U.S. 170 (1926); see also *Stratton's Independence* v. *Howbert,* 231 U.S. 399, 415 (1913).

Whatever there may be about a precise and scientific definition of "income," it imports . . . something entirely distinct from principal or capital. . . .[5]

These last two pronouncements of the Supreme Court appear in decisions dealing with the Corporation Excise Tax Act of 1909, but they have been reaffirmed in connection with the Sixteenth Amendment, the Court saying in *Bowers* v. *Kerbaugh-Empire Co., supra*:

"Income" has been taken to mean the same thing as used in the Corporation Excise Tax Act of 1909 in the Sixteenth Amendment and in the various revenue acts subsequently passed. *Southern Pacific* v. *Lowe*, 247 U.S. 330, 335; *Merchants L. & T. Co.* v. *Smietanka*, 255 U.S. 509, 519.

Further, it has been held that income does not include a return of capital or investment,[6] nor that portion of gross receipts necessary to be withdrawn in order to preserve intact capital used in producing those receipts;[7] that income must be new property acquired or increment detached from former capital or investment;[8] and that income is not limited to money receipts but may include property (other than money).[9]

8. The courts have held, however, that income does include realized gain on the sale of capital assets (*Merchants L. & T. Co.* v. *Smietanka, supra*). On this point the concept of income for United States tax purposes differs from that under the United Kingdom income tax and Canadian income tax.

9. The question whether in situations where there has been a substantial devaluation of the monetary unit, or a permanent depreciation in its purchasing power, there should be made adjustment for such change in the standard of measure in determining what portion of receipts constitutes a return of capital and what portion constitutes income has not been passed upon by the courts. However, if the courts should follow the implication of their decisions in *Bowers* v. *Kerbaugh-*

---

[5] *Doyle* v. *Mitchell Bros. Co.*, 247 U.S. 179, 185 (1918).
[6] *National Bank of Commerce of Seattle* v. *Commissioner of Internal Revenue*, CCA—9, 115 F. (2d) 875 (1940); *Commissioner of Internal Revenue* v. *Meyer*, CCA-6, 139 F. (2d) 256 (1943).
[7] *Doyle* v. *Mitchell Bros. Co., supra.*
[8] *Trust Co. of Georgia* v. *Rose*, 25 F. (2d) 997, aff'd. 28 F. (2d) 767 (1928).
[9] *Atkin's Estate* v. *Lucas*, 36 F. (2d) 611 (1929).

Empire Co., supra, and the principles announced in *Eisner* v. *Macomber*,[10] it is not inconceivable that the time will come when it will be considered too far from reality to indulge any longer in the fiction that the dollar is a constant unit of measure.

10. The Internal Revenue Code, imposing the Federal income tax, does define the term "net income" by way of setting forth in considerable detail rules for determining the amount upon which the tax is to be computed. However, such definition is limited by the meaning of the word "incomes" as used in the Sixteenth Amendment, although the Code's definition is actually narrower because of certain special deductions which it allows by way of congressional grace, such as specific personal exemptions.

There may be some difference of opinion as to what deductions from gross income are required by the Sixteenth Amendment in arriving at "income" as that term is used in the Amendment, and what deductions are merely a matter of congressional grace to be taken in arriving at the term "net income" as defined in the Internal Revenue Code. For example, in the case of mining companies whose business is to extract minerals from the ground it has been suggested that such companies are not necessarily entitled, in determining their net taxable income, to a deduction for depletion of such magnitude as to preserve intact the capital represented by the mineral they have extracted from the ground. Cf. *Stanton* v. *Baltic Mining Co.,* 240 U.S. 103 (1916); *Von Baumbach* v. *Sargent Land Co.,* 242 U.S. 503 (1917).

11. The entities for whom income is determined under the Code include individuals, estates and trusts, associations, corporations, and groups of related corporations. Partnerships are not regarded as entities to whom income is taxable, but the individual members of partnerships are charged with their distributive shares of the income received or accrued to partnerships. The period for which the income of each such entity is determined is a calendar or fiscal year.

12. The time for reporting income as prescribed by the Code is in general the year of receipt or accrual of the right to receive the money or property deemed to be income, including realization of gain on the disposition of capital assets, subject to the exception in the case of certain

[10] 252 U.S. 189 (1920).

types of exchanges where recognition of gains as taxable income is post-poned.

13. The time for taking deductions under the Code is in general the time when disbursements are made or the liabilities incurred, except that capital outlays are not allowed as deductions when made; but the deductions for capital outlays are required to be claimed when the assets acquired by such outlays are sold or as they are exhausted pursuant to rules for claiming depreciation or depletion or, in certain special cases, over a relatively short amortization period expressly provided for in the Code.

14. In determining certain points with regard to the reporting of income, claiming of deductions, measuring of costs, and interpreting of its provisions, the Code confers certain authority upon the Commissioner of Internal Revenue, subject to approval of the Secretary of the Treasury. Also it makes reference to good accounting practice as one of the guides to be followed in respect of certain points not specifically covered by the statute.

15. In measuring what portion of gross receipts from the sale or other disposition of property represents a return of capital, the Code has reference to their "cost." The Code also has reference to "cost" in determining the deduction for exhaustion of property, and in the case of sale or other disposition of property there is a provision for adjustment of such cost for certain changes in respect of the assets during the period while they were held, for example, for depreciation allowed or allowable in prior years.

16. In making adjustments of the cost basis of assets in determining gain upon their sale or other disposition, the Commissioner has ruled, and the courts have held, that such basis must be reduced by the depreciation claimed or allowable in respect of such property in each prior year even though there was no income in one or more of those years out of which a return of the capital might actually have been recovered.[11] The effect of this ruling may be that in respect of a particular asset a taxpayer may be taxed on a portion of the sales proceeds of such asset as income even though in reality it is a return of capital. This is contrary to the situation under the present Canadian income tax law.

[11] *Virginia Hotel Corporation* v. *Helvering,* 319 U.S. 523 (1943).

17. With regard to change in the unit of measure in determining "cost," the Code is silent. In practice it has been assumed that cost means the value in terms of dollars at the time the property in question was acquired, and that the dollar at the time of sale or other disposition has, or will be deemed to have, the same value as at the earlier date.

18. In the case of inventories, however, the taxpayer may elect, subject to certain conditions, to use the so-called "last-in, first-out" method (LIFO) in determining income derived from their sale. This has, to some extent, the effect indirectly of making adjustments for change in the value of the dollar. Where there has been a substantial depreciation in the value of the dollar, however, this method creates a potential future tax liability in respect of the normal stock of inventories which the taxpayer has on hand.

19. In the case of computing income from certain mining operations and the production of oil and gas, the allowance of depletion computed as a percentage of the sales price may also to some extent have the effect of making adjustment for change in the value of the dollar. But percentage depletion is usually regarded as a deduction dependent on legislative grace rather than as one required to arrive at "income" as the term is used in the Sixteenth Amendment.

20. Failure of the Code to provide in all cases for an adjustment of cost to take into account depreciation of the value of the dollar, that is, reduction in the standard of measure, has the effect of rendering the Federal income tax today in part a capital levy.

21. Some variation in the definition of "income" for Federal tax purposes is to be found in the excess profits tax law, which was in effect during World War II, and also in the new Excess Profits Tax Act of 1950, which was enacted in January 1951 as compared with the definition for normal tax and surtax purposes. The chief difference is that capital gains and losses, dividends received from other corporations, and certain other items are excluded for excess profits tax purposes.

22. Under the excess profits tax law, particularly under the Excess Profits Tax Act of 1950, the matter of currency devaluation or depreciation can be of material significance in determining the so-called excess

profits credit, which is used as the measure of "normal earnings." Such credit may be computed alternatively on the basis of historical invested capital (money or property paid for stock, plus borrowed capital) or so-called adjusted invested capital (present assets at their cost basis less liabilities plus borrowed capital) or base period (1946–1949) earnings; and failure to adjust for change in the value of money in measuring the invested capital or the base-period earnings may well result in understating the taxpayer's actual "normal earnings." There is no provision in the new excess profits tax law for any automatic adjustment for such monetary change in computing the credit; but it would appear that Congress has attempted indirectly to take into account the fact that the value of the dollar has depreciated during the past ten years, for in computing the excess profits credit based on invested capital Congress has allowed under the new excess profits tax law rates of return substantially higher than those allowed under the excess profits tax law of World War II. In explaining the provision for these higher rates, the House Ways and Means Committee, in their *Report on H.R. 9827* (the Excess Profits Tax Bill of 1950), at page 7, stated:

> It was believed necessary to provide for more liberal rates of return under your committee's bill than under the World War II law to allow for the general increase in rates of return on invested capital which has occurred since the pre-World War II period. Thus the rates of return were increased on the average by slightly more than 50 percent.

But this indirect approach has created inequities as between taxpayers, giving business with the more recently acquired assets a competitive advantage. Similarly, such congressional consciousness of the change in the value of the dollar over the last decade is reflected in their choice of the years 1946–1949 as the base period for determining the credit based on earnings under the new excess profits tax law in preference to 1936–1939, the base period under the World War II excess profits tax law. In this connection the Senate Finance Committee said in its *Report on H.R. 9827*:

> It was necessary to substitute the period 1946 to 1949 for the 1936 to 1939 base in your committee's bill both because of the large number of businesses which have been started recently and *because of the substan-*

tial changes which have occurred in the businesses currently in operation which were in existence in the period 1936 to 1939. [Italics supplied.]

23. With regard to the reconciliation of "incomes" of component entities subject to Federal taxation, it may be observed that the portion of receipts or other property of a corporation which is taxed to it as income is thereafter, less the amount expended in the payment of such taxes, regarded as capital in the hands of the corporation and not subject to further income tax to the corporation, but that upon distribution by way of dividends to the stockholders this same property is treated as income again for a second time and taxed as such to the stockholders. (In the case of a complete or partial liquidation of the corporation, the property distributed may be regarded as proceeds from the sale of the taxpayer's investment or a part of his investment, as the case may be, and he is then regarded as receiving income or capital gain only to the extent that the current value of property so distributed exceeds his cost for his stock.) This differs from the treatment of income passing through partnerships to individuals, which federally is not taxed to the partnership but to the individuals which are not, however, entitled to deduct depreciation in respect of partners' lives or to set up pensions for partners as corporations can for officers. It differs also from the treatment of income passing through trusts or estates, which is taxable either directly to the individuals, depending upon the conditions of distribution, or to the trust or estate, but not to both; for income which is taxed to a trust or estate is thereafter treated as capital for all purposes, and when distributed to the individual beneficiaries is not regarded as income to them but rather as capital. Moreover, this differs from the treatment accorded under the United Kingdom income tax law in respect of income passing through corporations by way of dividends to its stockholders, where the stockholders are allowed certain credits against their income tax for the income tax paid by the corporation in respect of that portion of its income so distributed. However, under the United States income tax law, in the case of dividends passing from one domestic corporation to another, the duplication is to some extent eliminated by the provision for a so-called "dividends received credit."

24. With regard to the reconciliation of "incomes" of the entities sub-

ject to Federal income tax with the national income, there has apparently been no serious attempt at reconciliation. For example, in the case of the Department of Commerce statistics on the national income by distributive shares, adjustment is made for inventory valuation, recognizing that reported profits, to the extent that they reflect merely a write-up in values owing to a change in the purchasing power of the dollar, are not in reality income; yet no such adjustment is provided for under the income tax laws except for such indirect adjustment as may result by a taxpayer's electing to use the LIFO method of inventorying.

Statutory Provision with Respect to Payment of Dividends

25. The law has at times been called upon to consider the meaning of "income," or alternatively of what may be considered "capital" as distinguished from income, in connection with statutory provisions restricting the payment of dividends by corporations under certain circumstances. Most of such statutes are phrased in terms of "forbidding impairment of capital" or requiring that dividends be paid out of "net profits" or "surplus." The general purpose of these statutes is to protect creditors and preferred stockholders, if any; and it has been suggested that they may also be intended to prevent deception of common stockholders who might easily assume that the dividends represented income.

26. In cases where the restriction on dividend payments is that capital may not be impaired, the courts have been called upon to determine what is "capital." For this purpose they have generally held it to mean an amount of money denominated as capital stock by the corporate charter or by the board of directors. This does not mean, of course, that for other purposes the actual capital of the corporation may not at the same time include money or property paid in as capital surplus or contributions to capital or earned surplus accumulated out of incomes of prior years.

27. Nor is measuring capital by reference to an amount of money, rather than by reference to particular assets, inconsistent with the purposes of a statutory restriction on the payment of dividends; for the creditors' claims are normally in terms of money, and this serves to give

notice to them of the margin of security they may expect as protection.

28. In determining whether or not capital is impaired, or in determining the amount of net profits of a corporation, it has quite generally been held that due allowance must be made for physical depreciation of assets. It also has been held that similar allowance must be made for depletion, but this is not necessarily so in all cases; and in certain states, such as Delaware, it is specifically provided in the statute relating to the payment of dividends that in the case of wasting assets corporations, such as mining companies, no allowance for depletion need be made.[12]

29. Moreover, where there has occurred extraordinary obsolescence or substantial decline in the market value of inventories, it has been required that such changes in value must be taken into account in determining whether a corporation's capital is impaired. And in at least one case, where under the Public Utility Law of the State of Wisconsin it was provided that a public-service corporation could not pay dividends while it was found by the Commission that its capital was impaired, it was held in a decision by the Wisconsin Public Utility Commission that radical decline in the price level should be taken into account in determining the value of the company's fixed assets for this purpose. The Commission said:

> Our summary investigation shows that the fixed capital accounts of this company were built up to a very large measure during a period of high prices, the properties being purchased and consolidations and financing effected on the basis of the then prevailing high prices. We are now in a period of much lower prices, and there is nothing to indicate that a period of relatively low prices will not persist for some time to come. This radical decline in the price level which has drastically diminished or wiped out values in many other lines of industry cannot fail to have an effect on the values of this company and all other utilities similarly situated. . . .[13]

30. Contrariwise, where the market value of the total assets of a corporation have appreciated substantially, it has been held in one of the leading cases on this subject, *Randall* v. *Bailey,* 288 N.Y. 280 (1942),

---

[12] Cf. also English cases on this.
[13] *Re Commonwealth Telephone Co.,* Wis. PUR 1932D 299 (1932).

that such appreciation may be taken into account in determining whether or not the payment of a dividend impairs capital.

Public-Service Industries Subject to Rate Fixing

31. Another field in which the law has had occasion to consider the determination of income is that of regulation of public utilities. Both Federal and state statutes grant authority to their respective governmental regulatory bodies to prescribe uniform systems of accounts, to lay down rules with regard to the form in which accounting information shall be presented in reports to the regulatory bodies, and to determine and fix the rates which the utilities subject to their jurisdictions may charge for their services. For example, the Federal Power Act provides:

> SECTION 301. (*a*) Every licensee and public utility shall make, keep, and preserve for such periods, such accounts, records of cost-accounting procedures, correspondence, memoranda, papers, books, and other records as the Commission may by rules and regulations prescribe as necessary or appropriate for purposes of the administration of this Act. . . . The Commission may prescribe a system of accounts to be kept by licensees and public utilities and may classify such licensees and public utilities and prescribe a system of accounts for each class.
>
> SECTION 302. (*a*) . . . The Commission may, from time to time, ascertain and determine, and by order fix, the proper and adequate rates of depreciation of the several classes of property of each licensee and public utility. . . .

32. Under the authority granted regulatory bodies to prescribe uniform systems of accounts, they have quite generally required utility companies to record their plant-investment accounts at the cost of those properties to the person who had first devoted them to public service, such cost being technically referred to as "original cost."

33. With regard to rate fixing, some of the regulatory statutes enumerate a number of different factors to be taken into account, and in general all provide that the rate shall be such as to afford a fair return on the utility company's investment. Thus the question of the determination of income frequently arises in rate-fixing cases along with the question how the capital investment is to be measured.

34. The regulatory bodies are allowed considerable discretion in such cases in providing how the capital shall be measured and income determined for these purposes, and the courts have indicated that they will not disturb such determinations by a regulatory body unless it appears that such determination is arbitrary or unreasonable.

35. In some of the earlier decisions of the Supreme Court, however, it was held mandatory that the reasonableness of rates should be determined upon the present fair value of the utility's properties, although various other elements, including original cost, were to be considered in determining the property values.[14] Similarly, it was held as a "settled rule" that the rate base was to be "present value," and that in determining income, for the purpose of ascertaining whether the utility was earning a fair return on its investment, the allowance for depreciation should be computed on the same present value basis.[15] In more recent cases the Court has refused to override determinations of the Commission basing rates on "original cost" of the properties and computing depreciation likewise on original cost in determining income.[16] Apparently the decision of the Supreme Court in these later cases was based on the view that under the circumstances the Commission's determination allowed the utility a fair return on its capital.

36. Under certain state law, notably Pennsylvania, for example, present fair value of the property is still the basis for rate determination.

37. As yet the question whether "original cost" should not be restated to reflect the substantial decline in the purchasing power of the dollar which has occurred during the past ten years has not been squarely presented to the courts in rate-making cases. However, were it presented and were the courts again to refuse to disturb a decision of the regulatory body determining rates on the basis of "original cost" without adjustment for change in the value of the dollar, such decision would not necessarily mean that the courts disapproved such adjustment in determining income for other purposes. What the courts would be deciding would be whether the rate determined by the Commission in the light of all the circumstances afforded the utility a fair return on

[14] *Smythe* v. *Ames*, 169 U.S. 466 (1898).
[15] *United Railways* v. *West*, 280 U.S. 234 (1930).
[16] *Federal Power Commission* v. *Hope Natural Gas Co.*, 320 U.S. 591 (1944).

its over-all investment. In the case of a utility whose properties were financed in part by the issuance of fixed money obligations, public authorities might argue that, for the purpose of determining a return on its investment now generally determined on an over-all basis, no adjustment for the change in the value of the dollar need be made in measuring its return of capital, since none would be made in measuring the capital which it must return to its creditors.

Corporate Reports

38. A corporation may not necessarily be required by law to make annual reports to its stockholders of its assets and liabilities and of its income, yet when a corporation or its directors undertake to issue such reports, although voluntarily, the corporation or its directors or both may well assume responsibility for the reports' not being misleading. The question may then arise whether an income statement, whether so labeled, or whether designated by some other caption, such as "Results of Operations," might be regarded as misleading if it fails to make adjustments for changes in the value of the monetary unit in which its accounts are stated.

39. In connection with the sale of securities by public offering, the Securities Act of 1933 in general requires the issuer to prepare and submit financial statements as part of the Registration Statement which it must file with the Securities and Exchange Commission, and to include financial statements in the Prospectus which it is required to issue. The Act also gives the Securities and Exchange Commission authority to promulgate rules and regulations defining "accounting" terms as used in the Act, and further authority to prescribe the form in which statements shall be submitted. For example, Section 19(a) of the Act provides in part:

> Among other things, the Commission shall have authority, for the purposes of this title, to prescribe the form or forms in which required information shall be set forth, the items or details to be shown in the balance sheet and earning statement, and the methods to be followed in the preparation of accounts, in the appraisal or valuation of assets and liabilities, in the determination of depreciation and depletion, in the differentiation of recurring and nonrecurring income, in the differentiation

of investment and operating income, and in the preparation, where the Commission deems it necessary or desirable, of consolidated balance sheets or income accounts of any person directly or indirectly controlling or controlled by the issuer, or any person under direct or indirect common control with the issuer; . . .

And the Act imposes broad liability upon the issuer, and, subject to certain defenses, upon underwriters and others, for misstatements of material facts or omissions to state material facts required to be stated, in registration statements or prospectuses, or omissions of material facts necessary to make the statements therein not misleading.

40. Moreover, all corporations whose securities are registered on a national securities exchange are required to file annual financial statements both with the exchange and with the Securities and Exchange Commission. The 1934 Act also gives the Commission powers with regard to prescribing the form of reports similar to the powers granted the Commission under the 1933 Act.[17] It also provides in substance that any person who files a report or document which is false or misleading as to a material fact shall be liable to any person who purchases or sells securities at a price which was affected by such statement unless the person filing the report or document shall prove that he acted in good faith and had no knowledge that such statement was false or misleading.

41. With regard to the issuance of financial reports to its stockholders in the case of corporations subject to the jurisdiction of the Securities and Exchange Commission under the Securities Exchange Act of 1934, the Commission has issued regulations with respect to solicitation of proxies requiring the corporations to provide an annual report to its security holders prior to the solicitation "containing such financial statements for the last fiscal year as will, in the opinion of the management, adequately reflect the financial position and operations of the issuer." Such reports need not necessarily be in the same form as the annual reports required to be filed with the Commission.

42. As yet, neither generally accepted principles of accounting nor any rules or regulations issued by the Securities and Exchange Commission require that a corporation should make adjustment in determining its income, or in any part of its financial statements, for changes in the

[17] E.g., Section 13(*b*) of the 1934 Act.

value of the dollar. In view of this, it would seem that at the present time the decision of a corporation or its directors not to make such changes in the financial statements which they issue should not be regarded as rendering the financial statements misleading so as to subject the corporation or its directors to liability to stockholders or others on such ground. However, it may be well to bear in mind that, if and when the question is ever presented to the courts, they may, with the benefit of hindsight, particularly if the purchasing power of the dollar continues to decline, inquire whether accountants were justified in clinging to accounting conventions adopted in the past during periods of relative price stability.

Other Situations

43. Other situations in which the law may be called upon to consider the determination of income include a wide variety of legal relationships. Among these are the valuation of goodwill and of the fair market value of shares of stock by capitalizing earnings; the matters of apportioning corporate distributions between life beneficiaries and remaindermen; of determining the legality of securities as investments for institutional investors; of determining claims for dividends on noncumulative preferred stock; of making payments of interest on income bonds; of determining net income for profit-sharing plans; of ascertaining the amount of funds available to an issuer for the purchase of its own stock; of complying with restrictions in indentures and charters, such as those with respect to the issue of new or additional securities or the declaration of dividends; and many others.

Summation

44. As indicated above, the pronouncements of the courts in the matter of determining income are to be judged in the light of the particular circumstances under which the question in each case is presented to the courts for review. In most instances the courts are not being asked to say what the concept of income should be in the abstract either from the standpoint of the economic welfare of society and its members or from the standpoint of what is good accounting; rather in most instances the courts are being asked to decide a dispute as to what par-

ticular persons had in mind when they used the terms "income" or "capital." Even in the case of statutory law, definitions of income set forth by the lawmakers should be viewed as designed to accomplish the purposes for which the statute was enacted rather than to lead our thinking in the science of political economy.

45. Moreover, it should be borne in mind that the law's pronouncements on the way in which income should be determined reflect in large measure the thinking of persons who in their relations with one another or with the State are concerned with such matters. Since the problem presented by the decline in the purchasing power of the dollar is still relatively novel, such thinking has not yet crystallized as to the adjustments which may be required as a result of such monetary change. Most of the pronouncements of the courts and of the statutes with respect to the determination of income have so far quite naturally reflected the thinking on the subject which developed during an era when both the dollar and the pound sterling were at least generally believed to represent relatively constant standards of measure, and when, on the basis of past experience, it could be expected that fluctuations in the general price level would consist of alternate upward and downward movements so that the secular, as distinguished by the cyclical, trend in the price level would remain stable.[18]

46. When, in view of the changed conditions existing today, thought does crystallize on this subject of the effect of change in the value of the monetary unit in the determination of income, it may then be expected that the law will reflect such thought. Undoubtedly Congress and others

[18] For example, Keynes speaks of the price level in England as being relatively stable from the end of the Napoleonic Wars in 1826 to the outbreak of World War I in 1914, with approximately the same level of price ruling in 1826, 1841, 1855, 1862, 1867, 1871, and 1915, and with deviations from such level seldom exceeding 30 per cent in either direction. Except for the temporary Greenback inflation in the Civil War, the situation in the United States appears to have been much the same. It is true that this relative price stability which had existed for nearly a century in the two great Common Law countries was broken by the extreme price fluctuations occasioned by World War I, but by 1926 the dollar at least appeared to have found a new level promising future constancy; and until World War II faith in such promise seemed to be justified. It is interesting to note that while prices in the United States and in the United Kingdom were still influenced by the gold standard's control on monetary values, the wholesale price indices in both countries, with the aid of the depression of the early 1930's, did in 1932 return to approximately their pre-World War I levels. The control of the gold standard on prices was, of course, removed when both countries abandoned the gold standard, the United Kingdom in 1931 and the United States in 1933, though the effect on prices was not immediately felt.

responsible for statutory law could assist, and perhaps lead the way by amending existing statutes, especially those relating to taxation of income, so as to make sure that what is reported as income is income in fact and does not include what in reality is capital. However, in the meantime and in the absence of such leadership from Congress, businessmen could do much toward this same end by adopting and establishing in their relations with one another reforms in accounting practice which will help in distinguishing that portion of our wealth which constitutes capital from the portion constituting income, with a view to maintaining the former intact and limiting our consumption to such portion of the latter as is not needed for the continued growth and expansion of our productive facilities.

47. While the reluctance of many businessmen to adopt accounting reforms which would adjust costs to reflect depreciation in the purchasing power of the dollar may be ascribed in part to their willingness to take full credit for the tremendous increase which reduction in the value of the dollar has caused in their gross dollar volume of sales and in their reported net income, there are certainly other, more valid, reasons for proceeding cautiously in discarding the old accounting practice of ignoring changes in the value of the dollar. Among such more valid reasons is the fear that to reform accounting in this respect would mean adopting a principle which, if we should ever enter into another era of falling prices, appreciation in the purchasing power of the dollar would require businesses to write down below their dollar cost the value at which they carry their assets on their books and in their balance sheets, while their borrowings could not be correspondingly written down because the liability to repay such borrowings is measured in dollars regardless of purchasing power. If those borrowing are relatively large, having been increased during the period when the dollar was depreciating because it then took more dollars to finance inventories and new construction, the adjustment of costs to reflect a subsequent appreciation in the value of the dollar would make the values at which they carry their assets look out of proportion to the dollar amount of their debt, and might well adversely affect their financial position, their ability to pay dividends, and so forth. This, however, should not be an insuperable problem. The most pressing

need right now for accounting reform concerns the effect of inflation on the determination of income. It should be possible to begin our reform by adjusting costs merely to reflect depreciation in the value of the dollar, and not appreciation, because today the long-term trend in the purchasing power of the dollar, at least as judged by the experience of the past eighteen years, has been merely in one direction—downward. Moreover, we might at first limit the application of such reform to the income statement, adjusting costs to reflect depreciation in the value of the dollar merely as and when those costs are matched against revenue in determining the income for a particular year. This would, of course, include the portion of costs representing exhaustion of assets attributable to such year, and not only tangible assets, the exhaustion of which is physical or due to obsolescence, but also intangible money assets, such as cash, accounts receivable, bonds, and so forth, the depreciation in value of which is occasioned directly by the depreciation in the value of the dollar.

SECTION 8

Summary and Conclusions

1. The ideal concept of business income for a year would be (*a*) useful for the major purposes for which income determinations are employed, (*b*) readily capable of being implemented, and (*c*) in reasonable conformity with concepts of other types of income. There are at least seven elements requiring consideration:

> The general concept
> The basis of measurement
> The medium of expression
> The major uses of determinations
> The methods of allocation in time
> The entities to which income is to be attributed
> The means of implementation.

2. The present study has needed to concern itself with implementation only to the extent that it affects the feasibility of a general concept or the usefulness of determinations for various purposes. It has been possible to narrow the subject also by considering the corporation as the typical accounting entity, and by giving merely passing consideration to corporations which deal only in money claims; consideration of special cases may be left to accountants as problems of implementation. As a practical matter the *medium of expression* must in general be the monetary unit in current use. In these ways the number of elements requiring consideration is reduced to four: the general concept, the basis of measurement, the major uses of determinations, and the methods of allocation in time, that is, between years.

3. In law and accounting there is agreement that business income is in general realized gain, that is, the gain derived from realized revenues; what constitutes realization, and what exceptions, if any, to the general

view should be recognized may be regarded as problems of implementation. Economists might disagree with the accounting view; accountants might agree with the economists that a gradual recognition of revenues on the basis of accretion might be theoretically preferable, but they might reject it as too seldom capable of implementation.

4. Gain is the excess of revenues over what may be broadly called "costs." Ideally, costs should be measured by standards as nearly identical as possible with those by which revenues are measured. As a practical matter, the choice of units of measurement seems to lie between *monetary units of changing purchasing power* and *units of equal purchasing power* such as that of the dollar of the year for which the income is being determined. If one could as readily be put into practice as the other, the latter would obviously be the more widely useful; but the former has in its favor its ease of application and its wide present-day acceptance.

5. The first choice is implemented by measuring the past cost of the goods or services, or the portions thereof, that have gone into the creation of the goods and services sold or whose useful life has been exhausted as an incident of the operation of the business simply in terms of the number of dollars as and when expended in acquiring or producing such goods or services.

6. The second choice may be implemented (1) by applying to the unadjusted cost figure determined in the first case an adjustment for the change in the purchasing power of the monetary unit, or (2) by using instead the cost of replacing or restoring what has been consumed, sold, or has gone out of existence.[1]

7. The last-mentioned basis has long been used in Great Britain by enterprises, such as railways, that were considered permanent. The LIFO method of accounting, the use of which in the United States was first permitted for tax purposes to a limited extent in 1938, and which has since been greatly extended, may partake of the characteristics of the last two alternatives. In Great Britain the LIFO method as such has never been accepted, although methods in some respects comparable have gained a very limited recognition.

8. With the exceptions indicated, "past monetary cost" has prevailed

---

[1] See Comments by Clark Warburton, p. 128.

as the basis of measurement of the charges against revenue both in the United States and in Great Britain. However, the justification for the acceptance of this basis has rested largely on the view that, subject to fluctuations over relatively short cycles, the monetary unit might be considered to be reasonably stable. When this condition exists (or where only dealings in money claims are involved) the difference between the results that would flow from the adoption of the two methods would not be important, especially over a period longer than a year.

9. The first major issue for consideration of the Group is, then: What changes in practice are called for where the assumption of reasonable stability is regarded as unwarranted?

10. Upon this point it would seem that in the longer view methods could, and should, be developed whereby the framework of accounting would be expanded so that the results of activities, measured in units of equal purchasing power, and the effects of changes in value of the monetary unit would be reflected separately in an integrated presentation which would also produce statements of financial position more broadly meaningful than the orthodox balance sheet of today. It is believed that statements of business income in which revenues and charges against revenue would be stated in units of substantially the same purchasing power would be significant and useful for many of the purposes for which income determinations are commonly used, if not also in reports upon stewardship.

11. The problem of presenting both the most generally useful income determination and a fully significant statement of financial position would doubtless present difficulties, but probably none which the highly developed accounting techniques of today could not solve.

12. For the present, it may well be that the primary statements of income should continue to be made on bases now commonly accepted. But corporations whose ownership is widely distributed should be encouraged to furnish information that will facilitate the determination of income measured in units of approximately equal purchasing power, and to provide such information wherever it is practicable to do so as part of the material upon which the independent accountant expresses his opinion.

Allocation Between Years

13. The two major problems (other than those of implementation) that arise in relation to allocation are, first, the assumptions that are to be made concerning the future, and second, whether, and if so how, any adjustment should be made of estimates and assumptions on which income was determined in the past.

14. Upon the first, the postulate of indefinite continuance seems to the Group to be acceptable in the large area in which it is now commonly accepted. There would seem to be need for fuller consideration by the accounting profession of the cases to which the postulate is not properly applicable or in which it has ceased to be valid.

15. The second point will be discussed in relation to uses of income determinations, but would seem to involve only a question of *form of presentation*.

Implementation

16. In putting accounting concepts into practice, there is a constant conflict between the objectives of increasing significance and lessening the variety of practices. The public should not underrate the extent of the existing varieties of methods. The accounting profession is constantly endeavoring to narrow the range of variety in different areas; but wars, social changes, high taxation, and marked changes in the price level are creating new problems which are dealt with in different ways.

17. The Group believes that in order to impart to accounting reports of income their maximum significance and usefulness, and to expedite the elimination of undesirable methods and the approach to uniformity, more systematic disclosure of the methods of dealing with elements of income determination is called for.

18. Notwithstanding the great advances in recent years, the extent of disclosure in annual reports still varies from corporation to corporation. More uniform disclosure is made in reports to the Securities and Exchange Commission, but these are not easily accessible to the average stockholder.

19. The Group considers that the proposal developed by the American Institute of Accountants and the New York Stock Exchange in the

years 1932–1934 contributed substantially to the improvement of financial reporting in the ensuing years and can well be applied to the present problem.

20. Managements must continue to accept the responsibility for choosing from among accepted methods of implementation those accounting methods that shall be adopted by the corporation under their management. The independent accountant should continue to recognize an obligation to pass upon the appropriateness of the methods employed and the fairness of the manner of their application in determining the income reported, and should assume a similar responsibility in respect of the supplementary information which forms a part of the material on which he passes.

21. There have been, and should continue to be, systematic efforts to attain a closer approach to uniformity in the treatment of routine transactions and to eliminate variations in practice which do not reflect material differences in postulates or conditions. Accounting will no doubt remain a compromise between theoretical and practical considerations.

Uses of Accounts

22. It is manifest that no single method of implementation of a single concept of income can in itself meet all the needs of those who use income determinations as a guide to action of one sort or another. The point that income is defined differently for different purposes emerges from any discussion of economic, legal, or accounting history of the problem.

23. If the purpose is to determine what payment should be made in respect of a year for income tax, or interest on an income bond, or management compensation, it may be appropriate to exclude what has been treated as a factor in determining income in the past and to compute income for the Nth year as the income for N years less what has been treated as income for the previous N minus 1 years.

24. If the purpose is to ascertain the shares of a year's products of industry that have been received by capital and labor respectively, past errors or failures of anticipation in previous years (other than normal overlaps) are significant only as a reminder that all current determina-

tions are, by their very nature, tentative and made in the light of the best knowledge of the time.

25. To the new investor, reports of income based on costs far below present replacement prices are of limited value. Such statements of earnings constitute in effect reports of stewardship, which are retrospective; the new investor is interested in present prices and future income.

26. The view may fairly be adopted that the investor who purchases stock from a previous holder steps into the latter's shoes; taxation of dividends is based on this view. But this view cannot be taken when he buys (otherwise than by succeeding to the preemptive rights of a stockholder) a new issue of stock made by an old company. For these reasons the income presentation that is appropriate in an annual report may not be as useful as some other presentation in a prospectus for the sale of stock.

27. Quite apart from this case there are changes in stock ownership which are so sweeping as to make effective cost to the new owner a more significant measure of accountability for property thereafter than cost to the corporation. It is not a part of this study to examine the problem in detail, but its existence and the question whether it has been adequately considered in accounting call for mention here.

28. The annual financial statements of corporations are primarily reports of stewardship, and the methods of presentation should be determined with constant regard to that primary purpose; but when corporations seek the advantage of marketability for their securities they incur an obligation of disclosure to investors generally.

29. It is highly desirable (as the tax statutes recognize) that income should be determined for income tax purposes and for general financial purposes as nearly as possible in the same way. This does not, of course, apply to provisions of the tax law which relieve a part of income from taxation as a matter of policy.

30. A further conclusion is that there is need for further study of concepts of income in relation to accounting entities, the corporation, the group of corporations, the enterprise, the ultimate beneficiaries (stockholders, and so forth). There is today no agreement on such questions as what *changes* in these entities should be deemed to call for the adoption of new "bases of accountability." Questions of this type should be

considered not only by accountants, practicing and academic, but in conjunction with lawyers, economists, and others.

As an incident to such studies the terminology in relation to income as used in different disciplines might be harmonized and improved. It would, for instance, be a great advance if agreement could be reached on a substitute for the word "value" and its derivatives to describe a monetary ascription carrying no connotation of actual worth, a usage common in business and accounting practice. The increased importance of the part played by income determinations in the economic life of the nation calls for much broader and better integrated consideration of such questions than they have hitherto received. Joint conferences between lawyers and accountants in relation to taxation have already been established; the scope of joint activities should be greatly broadened.

SECTION 9

Comments and Dissents

Dissent by GEORGE D. BAILEY

I regret that I am not able to assent to parts of the document in its final form. The deliberations of the Group, the monographs prepared for its information, and the discussions which the very existence of the Group has brought about have been of the greatest value to the members of the Group. The monographs which have been published and the report itself should be most provocative and helpful to accountants and others who deal with financial statements, and who are seeking a sound solution to the accounting aspect of the problems created by major changes in price levels.

My principal disagreements with the section entitled "Summary and Conclusions" are these:

1. I believe that Paragraphs 10, 11, and 12, when read in conjunction with Paragraphs 20 and 21, may be interpreted as proposing that publicly owned companies proceed forthwith to include data within their published financial statements or in notes or supplementary material attached thereto that will "facilitate the determination of income measured in units of approximately equal purchasing power." I believe that such ultimate goal or objective merits the most serious consideration and extensive experimentation. However, I believe that such paragraphs may also be read as proposing that the public accountant, reporting upon such statements, should at once include such data within the scope of the material on which he is to express his opinion. I do not believe that there is presently any such agreement on the practical methods by which to accomplish this objective as would enable an accountant to say that the data were or were not "in accordance with generally accepted accounting principles." Nor do I believe we are at a point where a company

should feel required to include such data. Instead, I believe there must be a period of voluntary experimentation with the preparation and publication of such data quite outside the financial statements. Inclusion of this data in the framework of the financial statements upon which the accountant expresses his opinion will become desirable if, and only if, by experimentation outside such framework some generally acceptable and practical procedures are developed.

2. There are two possible inferences that might be drawn from Paragraphs 22 through 28 with which I cannot agree. First, to the extent that financial statements are "reports on stewardship" they must present data to permit judgment on stewardship, including both how much has been built up and how well the stewardship has been performed. That implies a continual sharpening of concepts of income so as to permit better comparisons of progress between companies. These paragraphs might be read as encouraging disclosure of methods followed as an alternative and more desirable procedure, and from any such implication I must dissent. Second, there may be drawn from these sections the conclusion that the Group believes that financial statements as now generally prepared or published are improper, or that accountants are to be criticized for having said in their opinions that such statements "fairly presented, in accordance with generally accepted accounting principles, the financial condition and results of operations" of the companies involved. I want to disagree as positively and strongly as I can with any implication of this kind. I do not believe the Group individually or collectively would subscribe to any such conclusion. Nor do I believe there is today, or will be in the near future, any generally held belief, either among accountants or among other groups, that financial statements, such as are now customarily published, should be regarded as improper or incorrect.

The implications of the various sections are clearly that treatment of accounts, in view of the changing price level, is merely predominantly an income matter. I believe that the problems created are equally balance-sheet problems, and that they involve, as well, accumulative effects of price changes prior to the present. There is more than the theoretical problem of measuring all items of the income statement in monetary units of the same purchasing power; there are problems of providing for replacement, which again means recognition of obsolescence and technological improvements, points which are highly practical, and which reflection of only changing purchasing power does not touch upon.

In any event, the use of index figures to measure changing values of the monetary unit has not been sufficiently explored to suggest that such an easy way is accurate as well.

I believe that it would have been preferable to present only the "Introduction" and the "Summary and Conclusions" as the report of the Group, and to have presented Sections 2 through 7 as an appendix or supplement representing a statement of the general matters considered by the Group or an outline of the general course of discussion and argument on which the conclusions rested, particularly since there are many observations as to matters of history, of economic philosophy, or of law on which I do not feel competent to express any opinion. While I believe that Paragraph 18 of the "Introduction" specifically restricts the responsibility involved in signing the report to agreement with the "Summary and Conclusions," I wish, nevertheless, to dissent generally from any parts of Sections 2–7 which are inconsistent with the views expressed above.

Finally, I am not ready to accept the desirability of the basic theory of reflecting the changing value of the dollar until I can see some implementation thereof that will not be more harmful to adequate corporate reporting than to remain with present procedures.

Dissent by SOLOMON BARKIN

The report properly concludes that the determination of income is a "political question," meaning thereby an issue over which the various economic interests have differing approaches. It cannot therefore be resolved by accountants, economists or lawyers who are truly technicians for implementing agreements reached by the economic interests. The basic disposition underlying this report is reflected in the recommendation that to "management should be left the responsibility for choosing" the methods of accounting "from among accepted methods" (Paragraph 20). To this we must take exception. They must be the product of an agreement reached among all interested economic groups, including the trade unions.

We must also take exception to the fundamental recommendation contained in Paragraph 10 proposing the integrated financial statement to measure past financial transactions adjusted for fluctuating prices and thereby separate out the effects of the changing value of the monetary unit. The body of the analysis does not appraise the effect of this proposal upon the various groups whose economic fortunes may be affected by the accounting of the enterprise. One must also take exception to the selected nature of the materials and interpretations presented in the technical sections in support of the conclusion as providing an inadequate appraisal of the merits and failings of the proposal and their likely effects upon our business structure.

We do approve of closer uniformity in the treatment of the routine transactions but also urge that fuller agreement on the basic principles and methods among the interested economic groups is imperative. Greater uniformity in the accountings of operations in specific groups of industries would greatly advance the understanding and comparability of reports. Pending the consummation of this goal, we urged the closest adherence in reporting to the cost concept of accounting, and the minimum use of new techniques designed to increase charges on income. We whole-heartedly support the recommendation for the "more systematic disclosure of the methods" of income determination while the present variations exist.

The corporation, as the Committee on Accounting Procedure of the American Institute of Accountants declares, is "machinery created by the people . . . [to] serve a useful social purpose. . . . These results must be judged from the standpoint of society as a whole—not from that of any one group or interested parties." Management is only one party, and a very recent one, to the operation of the enterprise or corporation. There are many others including the directors, equity holders, minority interests, creditors, workers, communities and the nation. The accounting of the stewardship of this machinery must necessarily respond to the particular informational needs of each of these groups. To date, the degree of disclosure and the methods of accounting used by corporations have only slowly become more responsive to these interests, largely at the instigation of the stock exchanges and the Security and Exchange Commission. More parties and interests must share in determining the methods of principle and methods of accounting so that the final report will supply all with the data they each need for appraising the financial experience.

The report's crucial recommendations build on the assumption that the monetary unit has been considered reasonably stable and that the corporation must be maintained permanently by physical replacements equal in stabie monetary units to those which had been originally invested. Neither of these postulates as interpreted in this report can be accepted.

As for the so-called monetary postulate, it is a strain on one's credulity to presume that men have been blind to the sharp fluctuations in prices within each business cycle and over the century. While the last part of the nineteenth century (1865–1896) witnessed a long-time downward movement in prices, price variations were sharp within this period. Moreover this had been preceded and has been succeeded with alternating periods of rising prices (1790–1815; 1849–1869; 1896–1920; 1930–1951) and declining prices (1815–1849; 1920–1939). Within each period the fluctuations are wide and the trends among the commodities are diverse. We cannot accept the proposition that the monetary postulate rests on the stability of the price level. It is never really stable.

Part of almost every business transaction is a gain or loss resulting from good or bad timing with respect to price changes. It is true even in periods of rather narrow price fluctuations. The gains or losses are "real" in the financial sense.

Little support for the underlying recommendation can be obtained from the economist's interests, though the parallel is drawn in the report. His approach is national in scope; his definitions of income and production are necessarily different from those used by the businessman. When measuring "real" or physical production he is seeking to pierce the financial transaction. His definition of national production excludes the changing value of inventories resulting solely from price changes. To him it is not an addition to physical national product; but to the businessman it is a definite "financial gain."

A fuller exploration of Veblen's writings would have revealed that he was underscoring the conflict between "business" on the one hand and "industry" on the other. He was describing the differences between "acquisitive" and "creative" tendencies in our economy. The economist's efforts at measuring the "creative" results of "industry" cannot be reasonably used to support greater "acquisitions" by "business."

As for the second postulate, that of permanence, we must underscore that it has hitherto meant the maintenance of the original financial and not physical value of the enterprise. The technical sections abundantly illustrate the degree of departure proposed by the Group's proposals. Is not the practice to pay merely the face value of a debt sufficient confirmation of the position that it is only a financial replacement? Why should stockholders or more particularly the corporation enjoy the benefit of physical maintenance when no other claims in our economy enjoy this advantage in a period of rising prices or suffer the consequences in a period of declining prices? The risks of commercial transactions in our economy contemplate the acceptance of the risk in the variations in monetary values. They will continue to be accepted unless we grant all groups the same advantage. In which case we must contemplate the installation of a stable monetary unit of some type. But it appears that in the present era, our national economies place greater emphasis on full employment and progressive growth than on mere monetary stability.

The report recognizes the difficulties and inconsistencies resulting from the acceptance of the particular definition of permanence which it espouses. It seeks unsuccessfully to escape them through several inventions. One is the idea of using January, 1940, as the base date for all property. But much property was bought at higher prices during the first four decades of the century. A single general purchasing power index is proposed, but that has no real relevance to the value of capital goods. An even more difficult suggestion is that of using these indexes to measure the gains from price changes and those from advantageous timing of sales or purchases. The recommendations introduce elements of artificiality and discrimination and establish values unrelated to the business itself. The calculation of the stable value equivalence of an inventory or assets is a mathematical abstraction. In the case of physical assets, we know that most new items are not replacements of the same item but supplantations by new assets.

The discussion of the LIFO method proceeds on the thesis that it is a new concept of income. However, the technique has been constantly presented and was accepted by Congress as a more precise definition of the flow of goods and cost. The insistence that it, like the Excess Profits Tax Bill of 1950, represent new theories of income is a self-serving interpretation. If, as we believe, the LIFO method does not in itself introduce a new theory of income, there is no justification for demanding a change in the method of valuing physical assets. If there have been misapplications which have tended to strengthen the impression that a new theory of income has been created, then we should warn the users against, and urge the Bureau of Internal Revenue to resist, such abuse.

We recognize that price changes do make for the need of more careful evaluations of financial reports in so far as they are used for future judgments. The management may very properly supplement the regular statement with analysis of the cost of replacement of inventory and new capital. A new investor may desire to get an evaluation of the present value of the physical assets and inventory. In the same way, the other interests may desire information on the gains or losses during periods of declining prices and the savings made through the investment in new capital assets. In the era of increasing complexity of business transactions, the financial accounting must contain an increasing number of supplementary statements. Nor will business judgments be based solely on the financial report.

The adoption of the Group's proposals will compound the confusion which now prevails in financial reports, and which has made almost everyone wary about accepting them on their face value. Instead of multiplying the number of alternative principles and methods, we should restrict them and insist that the parties add on request such supplementary statements as will increase the reader's understanding and knowledge.

Three other observations in the technical sections of the report have also increased our wariness. It is proposed that smaller concerns be exempt from the privilege of following the principles enunciated in the Group's report since they would not have the technical competence to follow them. If the principles proposed by the Group have merit they should be universally applicable. Moreover, it emphasizes the basic query which the report raises as to whether the proposals will not accentuate the present tendencies for large firms to self-finance themselves out of profits and depreciation funds. This practice is making for larger enterprises, and accentuates the dangers of bigness. Are we in favor of accounting principles which encourage these trends when many laws seek to discourage them?

The Group's proposals run counter to the cost principles followed by regulatory bodies. The recommendations will increase the tension in that area and give heart to those who challenge the prevailing principles in their own self-interest.

Finally, the economic section suggests that the adoption of these principles would tend to reduce "business income taxes" and "wages" and "business investment." Are these the designed purposes for adopting these Group recommendations?

Dissent *by* CARMAN G. BLOUGH

While much of the report should be helpful in developing an understanding of the problems dealt with by the Income Study Group, I have been unable to cast my vote in favor of its publication because I feel that it does not give adequate recognition to the viewpoint of those members of the Group who believe we should adhere to the cost principle. Presentation of that viewpoint, it seems to me, is essential to a full understanding of the problem under consideration. Particularly, I feel that the report does not give enough recognition to the substantial arguments contained in the subcommittee report issued by Messrs. Greer and Wilcox, in which adherence to historical cost is favored and the adoption of a method of adjusting costs on the basis of index numbers is opposed.

Unless inflation should proceed so far that original dollar costs lose their practical significance, which I do not believe is yet the case, it seems to me that all of the procedures which have been proposed to date for reporting revenues and costs in units of equal purchasing power would result in so much confusion and misunderstanding that, under present conditions, it would be highly undesirable to use any of them.

It is also my belief that any method of accounting designed to meet the problems arising out of a changing price level, to be acceptable, would not only have to provide for the adjustment of inventory costs and the depreciation on fixed assets, but would also have to deal consistently with the other elements of the income statement and the amounts reflected in the balance sheet. Moreover, it is my belief that none of the index numbers that have been developed to date afford a sound basis for making accounting representations, although they may be useful in making statistical generalizations, and may therefore, when adequately explained, constitute a reasonable basis for presenting supplementary data.

While it is important to try to develop accounting procedures that will better meet the problems of inflation, it seems to me that it will be impossible to avoid losing a substantial part of the usefulness of our basic financial statements unless the procedures followed in their preparation are widely accepted. To avoid any such unfortunate result, it is my belief that experimentation with the development of new procedures of such a fundamental nature should be confined to the presentation of supplemental data apart from the basic statements until they have been developed to a point where they attain wide approval.

Accordingly, I should like to record my dissent from any portion of the report which implies that a general departure from the cost principle would be desirable at this time, or that any procedure proposed to date for adjusting historical costs to current costs is preferable to the historical cost principle, under current conditions; I must also take exception to anything in the report which might imply that it would be desirable to use the primary financial statements as the framework within which to experiment.

Comments by PERCIVAL F. BRUNDAGE

The report in its present form is a compromise between various points of view; suggestions have been incorporated in it from practically all of the members of the Group. As an individual I do not feel that it goes as far as I would like to see it go in approving and recommending that LIFO or market, whichever is lower, be used for inventory valuations, and that depreciation charges be converted to the current sales dollar by the use of index numbers. As the result of our discussions and study, I am convinced that statements of income which included large inventory profits in 1946 and 1947 and substantial inventory reductions in 1949 where LIFO was not used were less significant than they could have been made by its use. I also believe that depreciation charges should be related to the sales dollar.

It seems to me that by recognizing that we are in an inflationary period and recommending that it be taken into account for the future we are not in any way disapproving statements previously submitted in accordance with accepted accounting practice at the time. Furthermore, in my opinion, the difficulties involved in preparing statements of business income in which revenues and charges against revenues would both be stated in units of substantially the same purchasing power have been greatly exaggerated by those opposing it. Additions to plant account can be analyzed by years, the depreciation computed, as is now done, over the estimated useful life of such additions, and that charge converted by index numbers to dollars of the current year.

A general index like the Bureau of Labor's consumers' price index or its wholesale price index or some other index prepared for the purpose is, in my opinion, more suitable than a construction index, since we are not attempting to convert any particular unit into dollars but only to reflect changes in the general price level so that the dollars of income and expense will be roughly of the same size. I would not apply this principle to the balance sheet but would continue to show the plant at cost, the accumulated depreciation provisions on cost, and the additional provisions based on the index computation. I can see no point in constant revaluation of the plant account in the balance sheet. Yet part of the objection to the index-number proposal is that it would involve a restatement of the balance sheet at the end of each accounting period, a view which I cannot accept.

Comments *by* STEPHEN GILMAN

The report seems to suggest that LIFO (and, perhaps, accelerated depreciation) can serve either as a precedent for, or as a method of, income determination in terms of current dollars.

While both LIFO and accelerated depreciation may accomplish a desired effect on the income statement, they influence the balance sheet oppositely and, conceivably, below the limits of reasonable conservatism.

This effect contradicts our general thesis relating to decreased purchasing power of the dollar. It is inconsistent in that it provides "inflated" costs in the income statement and correspondingly "deflated" asset values in the balance sheet—a paradox which should cause concern to the certified public accountant who is requested to give as his opinion that his client's balance sheet presents fairly the client's financial position.

Comments *by* HOWARD C. GREER

The report makes a valuable contribution in proposing the expansion of the financial statements of large widely owned corporations to include a supplementary income calculation in which costs and revenues are measured in "units of equal purchasing power." A presentation of this type, to the extent that it can be set forth in agreed and understandable form, should provide a highly significant addition to the primary statement of "money income" which is accepted as the basic measure of the "earnings" of all ordinary business enterprises.

My concurrence in the report relates chiefly to this important conclusion, and to the accompanying restatements of established standards governing such matters as consistency, responsibility, disclosure, etc. It does not involve full acceptance of all the reasoning and argument presented in prior sections, which is in part an expression of the points of view of the official "consultants" of the Group, and not necessarily a reflection of the combined opinion of the Group itself.

This background material would be better balanced, and more nearly adequate, if it contained more extended references to such significant pronouncements as the summary of "Principles Underlying Corporate Financial Statements" published in 1935 by the American Accounting Association, and the regulations on statement presentation, issued from time to time by the Securities and Exchange Commission. These contributions to the development of acceptable measures of business income merit greater recognition than they receive here.

Since a major concern of the Group has been the insufficiency of "historical cost" depreciation charges to reflect current "value expirations" in periods of rising prices, further consideration might have been given to alternative cost-maximizing expedients such as accelerated amortization, charge-offs of fixed property replacements, etc. The analogy between LIFO accounting for inventory replacements and current "expensing" of plant and equipment replacements likewise might have been more clearly drawn.

The report would have been strengthened by avoidance of the disturbing implications in some of the phrasing that present-day financial statements obscure or misstate the facts of a situation, because they reflect past actual costs and realized money income, as opposed to "current purchasing power" costs and "economic income." It would be a gross injustice to accounting and accountants to encourage that view, or to let this document be regarded as a confession of sin or an apology for error.

Many, probably most, of the members of the Group continue to regard the measurement of "money" income from business activities as a useful and necessary task, and to attach importance to the difference between historical costs and current revenues, irrespective of changes in price levels. These members would not agree that the significance of such measurements rests on an assumption of "stability of the monetary unit," or that such significance has been nullified by any price fluctuations experienced or in prospect. The disclosure of a *further* truth does not invalidate one already discovered; it should rather create a broader understanding of the situation by throwing additional light on it.

If any other interpretation seems warranted by any of the language of the report, I wish emphatically to disclaim it as an expression of my views, which are more fully presented in the Proceedings of the Ohio State University Accounting Conference of May, 1949, and elsewhere.

Comments by GEORGE JASZI

I have not participated actively enough in the work of the Group to want to take a position on many of the issues discussed in the report. However, I agree with what appears to me the major, or at least a major, conclusion—namely, that from an economic standpoint it is more meaningful to express current costs in terms of current rather than past prices. In this connection I should like to make two comments. First, the LIFO method of inventory accounting secures a current valuation of inventories used up in production only when the physical volume of inventories is increasing. If the physical volume of inventories is decreasing the LIFO method fails to secure the desired current valuation. Second, I disagree with the suggestion of the report that an index of the general purchasing power of the dollar should be used to convert depreciation charges based on historical cost into current prices. I think that an index measuring the prices of capital goods—construction and equipment—would be more appropriate.

Dissent by EARLE C. KING

I disagree with the conclusions expressed or implied in the report, particularly in Paragraphs 10, 25, and 27 of Section 8, "Summary and Conclusions," that financial statements based upon historical cost, and which are not adjusted to reflect changes in purchasing power of the dollar, are inappropriate for, and of limited value to, investors. Such conclusions are, I believe, unwarranted and would lessen greatly, if not destroy completely, the confidence of the investing public in the many thousands of financial statements now in general use—statements bearing the certification of reputable accountants that they "present fairly the financial position . . . and results of operations . . . in conformity with generally accepted accounting principles. . . ."

I object to Paragraph 19 of Section 8 to the extent that the proposal of the American Institute of Accountants referred to therein may suggest that reasonable uniformity of accounting principles and methods of application is not to be regarded as a definite objective.

Dissent by A. E. LUNDVALL

I am in disagreement with the statements in the report which seem to imply approval of the desirability of reflecting the results of operations and financial position of business concerns in terms of current values and prospective costs instead of historical costs. Therefore, with respect to the "Summary and Conclusions," I particularly disagree with Paragraphs 4, 6, 10, and the last sentence of Paragraph 12.

In the interests of sound accounting, I believe that financial statements which have been adjusted to reflect estimated or theoretical costs should be an adjunct to and not a "part of the material upon which the independent accountant expresses his opinion." The substitution of the value concept for the cost principle in accounting is subject to abuse. With the rise in the price level following World War I, many business concerns followed the practice of having appraisals made of their properties in order to reflect in their accounts higher replacement costs. This practice was particularly prevalent in the Public Utility Gas and Electric Industry, and the abuses resulting from it led to a nationwide investigation of the industry by the Federal Trade Commission. That inquiry disclosed many practices of misrepresentation and deception in financial matters through unsound accounting practices as a result of the conversion of investment from a cost to a value basis.

Comments *by* HIRAM T. SCOVILL

I am voting in favor of publishing the report of the Study Group on Business Income, but I believe that the ideas presented in the report need exposure to many analytical minds in the related fields before being accepted as "weight of opinion." I have certain reservations which may be expressed as follows:

1. It is impossible in any large group of individuals engaged in a common pursuit to obtain unanimous recognition of a set of principles, code of operation, rules of procedure, or other important formal statement intended to guide or direct the actions of the individuals. Like most legislation, such guiding or directing statement must be a compromise.

2. If the compromise in the case of accounting matters tends to focus previously diffused ideas into a reasonably rational pattern and results in advising accountants in general of a highly acceptable and probably preferable procedure as viewed by men of unbiased judgment and broad experience, I am for such compromise.

3. If, perchance, the proposals of the Income Study Group as now drafted do not stand the test of continued and varied application, it is assumed that modifications can be made within a reasonable time. Just as progress has been made in the last forty years, so will progress be made in the next forty, the next ten, and the next five years. Our committee should not feel that it is so farsighted and so wise as to draft a document to stand unmodified for all time. We should present the best as we see it today, and assume that we or someone equally wise can effect necessary changes as needed, just as we have wrought changes in the patterns followed more or less loosely by our predecessors.

Dissent *by* CHARLES W. SMITH

I favor publication of the instant report as a provocative document, and because I believe it endorses, on the whole, the cost basis of accounting and financial reporting. However, there are certain statements in the report which seem clearly to sanction adjustments to income based upon the changing purchasing power of the dollar. I dissent from those statements.

Books must be kept in the established monetary unit. Any attempt to adjust the books to conform to the value of the monetary unit will likely result in a hodgepodge of practices that will not be beneficial either to our business institutions or to our national economy, in my opinion.

We are not altogether without some experience in the matter of stating depreciation expense on a value basis. The Supreme Court, in 1930, in *United Railways* v. *West,* 280 U.S. 234, a case with which I was associated, held that depreciation expense for the purposes of determining public utility rates and charges should be based upon the value of the utility property and not upon the cost thereof. That case originated before the economic crash of 1929. In the period following, the decision wholly lacked support in practice. In fact, there seemed to be general agreement in this period that the Supreme Court was in error. There was general relief, I believe, when the Court in *Federal Power Commission* v. *Hope Natural Gas Company,* 320 U.S. 591, another case with which I was associated, specifically overruled its holding in the United Railways case. The experience of attempting to deal with this matter when the fair-value doctrine of depreciation was the "law of the land" in respect to public-utility rate making convinced me that the value theory is wanting in principle and is unworkable in practice.

As I understand the report, the majority of the committee would sanction the stating of depreciation on a value basis with values arrived at by the use of general price-index numbers. This method is less refined than the replacement-cost theory which has been advocated in other places, and which is discussed in the report. Inasmuch as the replacement-cost theory is a more refined method, I will confine my main comments to it.

Under the replacement-cost theory an estimate is required of the cost of replacement of depreciable property at the time of replacement and when sufficient depreciation is accrued to equal the estimated new cost. The replacement-cost theory ignores wholly one of the outstanding facts of our industrial experience—one of the facts which has made

America great—technological improvement. The replacement-cost theory assumes that, technologically speaking, we replace old machinery and equipment in kind. Actually, we do not replace capital goods in kind but rather replace them with bigger and better things. An illustration or two, I believe, will make this clear.

The application of a special-purpose price index might show that an electric generating station built thirty-five or forty years ago would cost between two and three times as much today. No one with the slightest knowledge of electric generating stations, however, would say that such an old station is at all comparable with a new station built in, say, 1951. The old station would require an excessive amount of masonry and steel compared to the new station. The old station would probably require three pounds of coal to produce a kilowatt hour, whereas the new, modern station would use about nine-tenth of a pound of coal. On a capacity basis, that is, a kilowatt of capacity, the cost of the new station may not exceed greatly the cost of the old, and when the increased efficiency is taken into consideration may not cost any more at all. To force agreement with estimated replacement cost would, therefore, be arbitrary and erroneous. Certainly no one would buy a 1915 generating station at the old cost, if built today, in preference to a modern plant involving a higher outlay.

Not many years ago standard telephone cables consisted of numerous wires encased in a lead sheeting. In the present microwave era it would be just as wrong to apply replacement-cost index numbers to the cost of the old cable and call the result value for the purpose of arriving at depreciation expense as it would be to apply price-index numbers to the cost of the famous twenty-mule team and call the result the cost of automotive transportation. Such procedures deny the greatest attribute of our industrial behavior—technological development.

The replacement-cost or value theory contains another material error. Thereunder one item of expense, depreciation, is based upon the cost of currently made items of machinery and equipment, but other costs reflect the actual operation of the old items in spite of the technological changes which have occurred in the interim. This is an illogical admixture of the old and the new.

The application of a *general,* as distinguished from a special-purpose, index number compounds the wrong inherent in the replacement-cost theory. The use of a general price index assumes that all plant costs move in the same direction and to the same degree. Every student of prices knows this to be a fallacy. Some items may go down while others go up. Arbitrarily, however, they are all forced in line by the use of the general price-level index. The use of such an index, therefore, would not measure cost in terms of the dollars actually expended in the past or in terms of what the cost may be when replacement occurs. It is neither fish·nor fowl. Such a procedure may accrue as depreciation more or less than the dollars expended in the past or more or less than the dollars which may have to be spent when replacement occurs, if replacement is made. This kind of financial reporting geared only to the general price level, regardless of other important facts, cannot be very informative, in my opinion.

Utilities, in particular, under the investment principle of rate regulation, should adhere to the cost basis of stating depreciation expense. Under the investment principle of rate regulation, when the additional investment is made it is protected through the allowance of a fair return thereon plus full depreciation. This is a practical method in that it avoids guesswork and at the same time fully protects the investment, whatever it may be, when made.

If the fair-value doctrine is sanctioned, it may be anticipated that a hodgepodge of financial reporting will result. It is conceivable that some business enterprises would compute depreciation expense by adjustments geared to the general price level; others would employ a special price index, and others would adhere to cost. The great gains toward uniformity in financial reporting in the last fifteen years or so would be jettisoned if such multifarious practices were to prevail.

The accounting process is a poor and hopelessly inadequate tool to deal effectively with the economic evils of inflation and deflation. In fact, the application of this tool in the manner suggested in certain parts of the report would be harmful rather than helpful. At best only a few transactions can be adjusted to take cognizance of changes in price levels. The great bulk of business transactions will continue to be stated on the basis of the normal monetary unit. In my opinion we would accomplish much more by devoting our efforts to the prevention of inflation and deflation rather than by attempting, unsuccessfully, I suggest, to apply a palliative designed to soothe only one or two of the symptoms.

Comments *by* FREDERICK F. STEPHAN

I concur in the conclusions and recommendations set forth in the Report of the Study Group in so far as they pertain to informing investors about the effects of changes in the purchasing power of the monetary unit on the operations and income of corporations. I wish to dissociate myself from conclusions and recommendations concerning questions of law and, particularly, questions of taxation, such as Paragraphs 23, 24, and 29 of the summary section. The interests of bond-holders, long-term lenders, and employees with pension rights merit consideration on a par with those of stockholders when tax policy is modified to take account of gross changes in the purchasing power of the dollar. There are other fundamental considerations, beyond the scope of the Study, that make it unwise, in my opinion, to extend our conclusions beyond the problems of accounting and economic analysis.

Comments *by* CLARK WARBURTON

I subscribe wholeheartedly to the view that "costs should be measured by standards as nearly identical as possible with those by which revenues are measured," and that choice of a unit of equal purchasing power is preferable to the use of monetary units of changing purchasing power. However, the practicality of using an existing index number for implementation of this point of view is less real than is implied in Note 4 to Section 6 of the report.

For many specific years there is a great difference between adjustments that would be made on the basis of the two indexes mentioned which are currently available; namely, the cost-of-living or consumers' prices index and the wholesale price index of the Bureau of Labor Statistics. In the year 1950, for example (taking the figure for December in comparison with that for December of the preceding year), consumers' prices rose by 6 per cent while wholesale prices rose by 16 per cent. If the average figure for 1950 is compared with the average for 1949, consumers' prices increased by 1 per cent, while wholesale prices rose by 4 per cent. That is to say, choice of the latter index would mean an adjustment about three or four times as large as would be required by choice of the former index. Larger divergencies between the two indexes have occurred in some prior years.

The chief problem considered by the Study Group is that of charges for the exhaustion of property. Since practically all other items of revenue and cost, particularly if the LIFO method of accounting is used for inventories, are automatically valued on the basis of average prices for their respective components (i.e., specific types of goods or services) for the year covered by an income statement, no index so comprehensive as a cost-of-living or wholesale price index can be appropriately applied to charges for property exhaustion. If an index number is to be used for this item, as a correction of amounts estimated on the basis of original cost, the index should pertain to the types of property to which the exhaustion charges relate. This means an index of such items as construction costs and prices of producers' capital equipment. No such index is currently published, though several indexes of construction costs are available.

For another problem mentioned in the report but given less emphasis —that of adjusting "net income" figures for prior years for comparison with a current figure—a comprehensive price index is needed. However, for this problem neither the cost-of-living index nor the wholesale price index is as suitable as an index of the type recently prepared by the Department of Commerce as a result of its estimate of "gross national product" in constant dollars (*National Income and Product of the United States, 1929–1950*, p. 146). This type of index is not available on a monthly basis, and the annual figures are not likely to be published promptly enough to be used in the annual reports of corporations.

The suitability of index numbers needs more study before use of them can be recommended as an appropriate method of handling the problems of charges for property exhaustion and comparability of corporation income statements over a period of years.

Dissent by WILLIAM W. WERNTZ

I am unable to agree with certain parts of the report as presented to members of the Study Group on Business Income for their approval or disapproval. The report, as well as the monographs which have been developed for the guidance of the Group, should prove of the greatest value to the further development and consideration of concepts of business income. The comments which I feel called upon to make, with respect to certain portions of the report, are not to be taken as an indication of disagreement with the *ultimate* desirability of obtaining financial data in terms of units of constant purchasing power. If means can be developed to obtain this objective, the resultant figures should prove extremely helpful to stockholders and investors, as well as management. However, such data would, in my opinion, in no way supplant financial statements which reflect money income, but they should prove a very valuable adjunct to such statements.

As I understand Paragraph 17 of the "Introduction," signature of the report does not carry with it either approval or disapproval of Sections 2 through 7. These sections include statements of historical fact and developments, conclusions drawn from historical events or relationships, and observations as to matters of economic philosophy and law. Their scope is such that detailed verification or even critical comment by any one individual is scarcely feasible. On the whole, it would, I believe, be far preferable to treat Sections 2–7 as a general statement of various matters and opinions taken under advisement by the members of the Group rather than (as they may possibly be read in their present position in the report) as a statement of detailed arguments or logic relied upon by any individual member in arriving at his judgment as to the propriety of the specific conclusions in the final section. It would also have been preferable to confine the formal, signed report to the statements set forth in the introduction and conclusion, lest the specific and more detailed language of the intervening sections be construed by the reader as appropriate elaborations of certain of the conclusions.

There are, however, two matters as to which a comment seems desirable. Inferences or conclusions are drawn in Section 3 from accounting practice to the effect that the "realization postulate" and the "related cost principle" were either nonexistent or inoperative prior to 1913. I believe that the history cited is susceptible of a quite different interpretation and that it does not necessarily support this view. In this connection, an article in the October, 1951, *Accounting Review* by D. A. Litherland, entitled "Fixed Asset Replacement a Half Century Ago," seems to me to support my belief.

In Paragraph 77 of Section 3, there is the statement that the Securities and Exchange Commission "has not, however, up to now required the full scheme of disclosure of methods which was outlined in the recommendations of the Institute's (American Institute of Accountants) Committee in 1932, and which was an integral part of the procedure contemplated by the Institute and the New York Stock Exchange." To the best of my knowledge, there has been no authoritative utterance, in implementation of that recommendation, as to what constituted the "full scheme of disclosure of methods" then recommended. It is a matter of history, I believe, that in arriving at its requirements as to disclosure of accounting principles, as reflected first in Forms 10 and A-2 and later in Regulation S-X, the Commission and its staff had the benefit of the assistance and critical comment of many accountants and others interested in financial statements. It was, in my opinion, the belief of the Commission and its staff that observance of its disclosure requirements did result in a reasonably comprehensive statement of the major accounting principles employed by the subject companies. Moreover, in Regulation S-X, Rule 3.08 specifically suggests that such disclosure of methods followed be presented in the form of a "single statement."

The remainder of my comments deal specifically with the indicated paragraphs of the "Summary and Conclusions."

1. Accountants generally, and the Securities and Exchange Commission and other regulatory agencies, have always agreed that financial statements of commercial and industrial enterprises for use by stockholders and prospective investors may properly be based on cost without adjustment, as such, for changes in purchasing power and without collateral disclosure of items of income and expense, or of assets and liabilities, in terms of a constant unit of purchasing power. No methods

of portraying financial data in such constant units of purchasing power yet developed have received any general acceptance, or even any considerable use. There is, on the contrary, sincere disagreement as to what principles might or should be followed to arrive at income in terms of a constant unit. Accordingly, I believe that any statement or inference based on Paragraphs 10, 11, 12, 25, 26, 27, or 28, to the effect that financial statements in the form generally now in use are inappropriate without the added data mentioned above, is wholly improper and would not be supported by the Group.

2. I do not believe that, in the present state of affairs, accountants can properly be asked or required to include the suggested data within the scope of their reports. Instead, I think that inclusion of such data within the scope of the accountant's report can be determined to be desirable (or indeed undesirable) only after extensive experimentation outside of the present forms of financial statements and only after reaching of some general agreement as to the practicability of furnishing such data and as to the methods to be employed. This comment relates particularly to Paragraphs 12 and 21, and any contrary inferences which might be drawn therefrom.

3. Paragraph 25 is particularly susceptible to the implication that the cost statements now in general use are not desirable for the prospective investor. I believe, on the contrary, that they are useful, and that they should be the basic financial data furnished. Whether *supplementary* statements can be developed to portray financial data in units of constant purchasing power remains to be seen. Whether such data would be more or less useful to the prospective investor (as compared to a stockholder) is a question not free from doubt. In this connection the observations and arguments of Homer Kripke, in an article entitled "Accountants' Financial Statements and Fact-finding in the Law of Corporate Regulations," and published in the September, 1941, *Journal of Accountancy,* seem to be clearly pertinent, at least until means have been developed and agreed upon whereby dollar value changes, resulting from general price-level changes, can be clearly segregated from dollar value changes resulting from such factors as managerial decisions, technological improvements, or changes in the price levels of par-

ticular goods as distinguished from changes in the general price level.

4. I believe greater reference should have been made to the study prepared for the Group by Messrs. Wilcox and Greer, published in the *Illinois Certified Accountant* in September of 1950, and referred to in Paragraph 37 of Section 5 of the report. I also believe that reference should be made, and to my mind with approval, to several reports of the American Accounting Association, particularly that of its Committee on Concepts and Standards, entitled "Price Level Changes and Financial Statements," published in the *Accounting Review* for October, 1951. Finally, I do not believe a report of this type should fail to mention the book *Stabilized Accounting,* published in 1936 by Henry Sweeney, a leading pioneer in the field of accounting for price-level changes.

I am also, of course, unable to assent to language appearing elsewhere in the "Summary and Conclusions" or in the remainder of the report to the extent that it may be inconsistent with the views expressed above.

Dissent by EDWARD B. WILCOX

My dissent to the report of the Study Group on Business Income relates primarily to the subject of price level adjustments. Paragraphs 10, 11, and 12 of the section entitled Summary and Conclusions, set forth most, although not all, of the views with which I disagree in this connection. These views are that statements of business income in which revenues and charges would be stated in units of substantially the same purchasing power would be significant and useful for many purposes, that the accounting technique of today could solve the difficulties of such presentations, and that certain corporations should be encouraged to furnish such information and to include it in the framework of accounting statements upon which the independent accountant expresses his opinion.

Neither the significance nor the purposes for which the usefulness of such statements is claimed are specifically set forth, nor is there any clear understanding of the term "same purchasing power." From the suggested use of general price indexes it appears that this is to be stated by translating certain historical dollar costs into current charges on the basis of statistical averages of price changes unrelated to the type of costs to which they are to be applied, and regardless of related technological changes which would invalidate such blanket adjustments. It is clear from this and other conflicting proposals that no adequate method has yet been devised which justifies reliance in achievement of the regrettably vague purpose being sought. However highly developed the accounting techniques of today may be, they are not prepared to solve these difficulties. It is therefore improper to encourage any corporations to include such information in the framework of their financial statements upon which independent accountants express opin-ions. Such action would vastly minimize the usefulness of financial reporting, not only because of the vagueness of objective and the inade-quate means of attaining it, but also because of the inconsistency and confusion that would ensue. It is a truism that any figure representing annual net income is of limited significance; it would be a misrepre-sentation to claim added significance for such a figure adjusted by inadequately explored methods in the quest of a vague objective. These views are set forth more fully in the report which Mr. Howard Greer and I made to the Study Group entitled, "The Case Against Price Level Adjustments in Income Determination," referred to in the attached bibliography.

Whether or not price level adjustments should ever be brought into the framework of financial statements, the disadvantages of doing so in the United States at this time clearly outweigh any possible advantages. Primarily, statements of income and financial position should continue to be made on bases now commonly accepted. It might be useful, how-ever, for study and experimentation to continue in the development of information regarding the effect of changes in price levels, completely outside the framework of such statements. Such study and experimenta-tion would be appropriate both as academic and research projects and by managements in interpretation of current reports. While early proj-ects of this kind may have limited usefulness, they may lead to the development of methods which, at a later date, may be capable of wider application. More than this cannot be undertaken now without doing more harm than good.

It follows that my dissent also runs to those parts of the report of the Study Group on Business Income which I believe unduly disparage presently accepted methods and those persons who would adhere to them. I refer for example to Paragraphs 15 and 48 in Section 4 and Paragraph 25 in the Summary and Conclusions. Similarly, I believe it is not entirely fair to omit reference to the invaluable narrowing of areas of inconsistency in financial reporting which has been achieved in recent years.

Although it may be implicit, I wish to make it clear that my dissent applies not only to the specific paragraphs mentioned above, but also to all parts of the report which support or imply support of the matters in which I disagree. To cite and comment on all such matters in detail would require a dissent almost as long as the report itself. Large parts of the entire document are subject to this blanket dissent. I also wish to state that I am neither approving nor disapproving of any legal, economic, or historical portions of the report which I am not competent to judge, or which I have not had an opportunity to verify.

Comments by GEORGE O. MAY AND OSWALD KNAUTH

As the members of the Group who put together the first draft of the report, we feel we should comment briefly on the present text.

We should also note the appearance in the *Accounting Review* of October, 1951, of an important report by a committee of the American Accounting Association.

First, we must express our appreciation of the many constructive criticisms and suggestions offered by members of the Group, the adoption of which has greatly improved the report.

We agree with the opinion that modifications made in an effort to reconcile conflicting views have resulted in some loss of incisiveness in the conclusions. We think, for instance, that the Group should have recommended that in the case of railways and regulated utilities, provisions for exhaustion of property computed on the basis of current price levels should be made mandatory, as a matter both of good accounting and of sound economic policy.

However, an important result will have been achieved if the report leads to more general acceptance of the view that "business income" has two components which are separable and possess different significances, one reflecting the results of business activities measured in units of substantially equal purchasing power, and the other reflecting the results of changes in the purchasing power of the monetary unit on the final determinations of income.

Since the report goes no further, even in its recommendation of a "longer-view" objective than to advocate the separation of the two components, much of the dissent recorded seems to be unduly apprehensive or to disclaim approval of proposals that have not been made.

Whether eventually the first component alone should be deemed to constitute "business income" and a separate designation should be given to the second may be left for future consideration.

We feel that we should not comment on dissents which reflect differences of opinion, legal, political, economic, or accounting, that were to be anticipated when the report was being prepared, but we must discuss the suggestion that "it is not entirely fair to omit reference to the invaluable narrowing of areas of inconsistency in financial reporting which has been achieved in recent years."

It is an essential part of our view that, despite narrowing at some points, the area in question has been greatly widened in recent years as a result of social change, war, price inflation, and high taxation. This broadening is illustrated by the range of choice in allocation of so-called past service benefits under persion schemes to future years; by introduction, on an optional basis, of LIFO inventorying, based either on actual acquisition costs or on price indexes; and by accelerated depreciation; all of which are discussed in Sections 3 to 5 of the report.

Because of the widening of what may be called the "tolerances" in current income determinations, the differences in results of applying one price index or another in accounting for exhaustion of physical property (to which Mr. Warburton refers) do not seem to us of major importance, especially as property investment is normally spread over many years. For the same reason we regard the more systematic and explicit description of accounting methods in annual reports to stockholders as even more desirable now than in 1932 (Sec. 7, Par. 19).

*   *   *   *   *

We welcome the report of a committee of the American Accounting Association which has appeared since the draft of this report was circulated. To a large extent its views are in accord with those expressed by the study group. Thus the committee recognizes the desirability of inclusion in financial reports of "supplementary statements which present the effects of the fluctuations in value of the dollar upon net income and upon financial position." It suggests that those effects should be measured "in terms of the over-all purchasing power of the dollar." It does not regard the degree of error involved in the use of price indexes as a bar to their use.

The committee takes as its first premise a statement which differs from the view accepted in this report as to present accounting methods. It says:

> As traditionally measured, accounting net income expresses the excess of periodic revenue over the cost of the capital (resources) "consumed" in earning that revenue. Under the present monetary postulate the "costs" charged against revenue in measuring net income are, in general, the dollar costs—the number of dollars initially invested.

This statement is ambiguous, especially if the word "traditionally" is emphasized. It may imply that the committee rejects such recent developments as accelerated depreciation and LIFO accounting on a price-index basis. In that case its opposition to the inclusion of provisions for exhaustion of property based on price indexes within the material on which the accountant passes may be regarded as natural and consistent. But in that case it is assuming a system of determination of business income which, in our view, does not adequately reflect existing practice.

The committee takes the view that the first step should be experimentation by business managements in forms of exposition upon which the accountants should express no opinion, though they might assist in the formulation of them.

We feel that this position should not be accepted either by accountants or by the public. Accountants should neither assume to dictate nor be content to follow in such matters. They should lead, advise, and assist in implementation; and they should stand ready to express their opinions upon the fairness of any disclosure so far as matters within their competence are involved.

Fifty years ago "business income" was of little interest to any except those engaged in business or finance. Accountants could then rightly be guided in their concepts of business income by the views of businessmen. So, indeed, were the courts in both America and Great Britain, and the taxing authority in the latter country, in which income taxation was well established.

The American Institute of Accountants, in the letter to The Rockefeller Foundation, which is one of the charter documents of the Group (Exhibit I), recognized that interest in accounting concepts such as "business income" had been so greatly broadened that they must be conceived today "from the standpoint of society as a whole." "Business income" is now a concept of importance to the whole body politic.

We find it difficult to understand why an accountant who claims, and is presumed, to be competent to pass upon the fairness of a purely subjective computation of a charge for accelerated depreciation or of the application of LIFO accounting on the basis of price indexes should not be, or be expected to become, competent to pass also on the fairness of an application of a price index to a charge for exhaustion.

A more important difference of opinion is presented by the statement of the association's committee: "The measurement of price level changes should be all-inclusive; all statement items affected should be adjusted in a consistent manner." This would mean, we take it, that unless changes in the value of the dollar are to be taken into account in respect of purely monetary transactions they should not be taken into account in determining charges against revenues in respect of consumption of physical property, as they are at present, when LIFO is applied as the basis of price indexes, and as they were in measuring exhaustion of physical capital assets in the accounting of English railways prior to nationalization. Such a proposal seems to us to confuse two distinct objects and to be tantamount to rejection of the proposal of which the committee approves.

An "all-inclusive" adjustment would result, *inter alia,* in showing a loss rather than income as being derived from the maturing of a savings bond of $100 which had been purchased ten years earlier for $75 if the purchasing power of the dollar had fallen more than 25 per cent in the interval. Such a view is, we believe, politically impracticable. It is not, in our opinion, a natural or logical corollary of the proposition that dispositions and consumptions of *physical properties* in the course of business activities should be measured in units of the same purchasing power as the revenues in measuring income derived from those activities. This income itself would still be expressed in monetary units comparable with those in which other forms of income are measured.

The task of making statements of financial position more significant is one of difficulty and must be faced. It arises only incidentally in a consideration of "business income." But the method of joint study adopted for the first time in the creation of this Group might well be extended to it under the auspices of one of the foundations interested in the social sciences. We should question the wisdom of submitting to stockholders two complete sets of financial statements prepared on different bases and reconciled in detail, as proposed in the committee's conclusion No. 6.

The committee's views on the two points of differences should be no bar to its acceptance of the proposal made in this report that the two components of business income as now conceived (the results of activities measured in units of equal purchasing power and the results of changes in the value of the monetary unit) should be recognized as separable and possessing different significances, and that efforts should be made to isolate them, first in supplementary material, and ultimately, perhaps, in the primary accounts of business corporations.

EXHIBIT I

COPY OF LETTER TO THE ROCKEFELLER FOUNDATION
SETTING FORTH THE OBJECTIVES OF
THE STUDY GROUP ON BUSINESS INCOME

May 27, 1947

Social Science Division
The Rockefeller Foundation
49 West 49th Street
New York, N. Y.

Gentlemen:

The American Institute of Accountants hereby requests that The Rockefeller Foundation make a grant, to be administered by the Institute, of thirty thousand dollars ($30,000), to be available over a period of three years, for the purposes of a survey and a historical study of the uses of the word "income" and terms associated therewith in accounting and in business, economic, and political fields. The Institute is prepared to assume the administrative duties in connection with such a study and to provide the necessary office facilities. It contemplates that the general director should be an outstanding accountant. He would have associated with him an executive committee representative of various disciplines. Mr. George O. May, who was for many years director of the National Bureau of Economic Research, and is the author of "Financial Accounting" and the chairman of the Institute's committee on terminology, has expressed readiness to take an active part in the project.

The Institute has appropriated the sum of thirty thousand dollars ($30,000) from its funds to be available over the same period of three years, mainly for the compensation of the person in immediate and continuous control of the study. If the grant is made by the Council, efforts will be made to secure financial as well as personal cooperation from other bodies representative of other disciplines, such as the law,

Exhibit I 141

economics and statistics. In general, it is contemplated that there should be a small executive committee of perhaps seven members of the larger study group comprising representatives of various disciplines and professions, as indicated in the enclosed memorandum. Through the members of this group an expression of views of a still larger circle would, it is hoped, be elicited.

During the last third of the century, accounting has come to play a major part in taxation, regulation, and valuation; it has assumed new importance as a result of developments of recent years in relations between management and labor. The income statement, in particular, has grown in importance, and the desirability of securing the maximum unity of concept in this field is, the Institute believes, today apparent.

The Institute is deeply concerned over the ambiguities and uncertainties that attend the use of accounting terms and accounting statements, to some extent within the accounting field and to a larger extent in the field in which accounts are used. Recognizing a responsibility in the matter, the Institute, through its committee on terminology, has made a number of reports dealing with the terms that are most commonly used, such as balance-sheet, income, surplus, etc. It has been forced to realize that real progress can be attained only in cooperation with those who use accounts and those who use similar terms in their own disciplines. It contemplates the proposed study as a part of its contribution to the social welfare.

It would be too much to expect that the study would result in general agreement on senses in which the word "income" could properly be used. It would seem not unreasonable to suppose that a fair measure of agreement could be reached as to the proper usage of the word when combined with a particular clarifying adjective. The exchange of ideas in the course of an attempt to reach such a goal would in itself be of great educational value. The report, it is contemplated, would afford a greatly improved starting point for the determination of such important economic issues as the relation between business income, as now commonly computed, and real "ability to pay."

For the purpose of indicating more clearly the general nature of the Institute's objectives, there are attached hereto documents which show the steps which the Institute has taken in the past in the general direction of the proposed study, namely, correspondence with the New York Stock Exchange, 1932 to 1934; extract from the first bulletin of the research department of the Institute, 1939; and five bulletins containing reports of its committee on terminology, issued between 1940 and 1944 (Nos. 7, 9, 12, 16 and 20). There are also attached hereto an outline of the project and a brief statement of the suggested scope or method of the inquiry.

We shall look forward with interest to a report of the results of the Council's consideration of this matter.

Yours sincerely,

Signed   JOHN L. CAREY, Secretary

JLC:hh

enc.

Exhibit I 143

LIST OF THOSE WHO HAVE PARTICIPATED IN THE WORK OF THE STUDY GROUP

MEMBERS OF THE BUSINESS INCOME STUDY GROUP APPROVING REPORT FOR PUBLICATION OR SUBMITTING DISSENTS

Andrews, T. Coleman

Bailey, George D., see dissent, page 110.

Baker, Ralph J.

Barkin, Solomon, see dissent, page 112.

Barnard, Chester I.

Blackie, W.

Blough, Carman G., see dissent, page 117.

Briggs, Robert P.

Broad, S. J.

Brundage, Percival F., see comments, page 119.

Burns, Arthur F.

Dean, Arthur H.

Dohr, James L.

Fabricant, Solomon

Gilman, Stephen, see comments, page 120.

Goldsmith, Raymond

Greer, Howard C., see comments, page 120.

Gressens, Otto

Hagerty, H. C.

Hancock, John M.

Hargrave, Thomas J.

Haskell, John H. F.

Henderson, Alexander I.

Holme, Stanley A.

Jarchow, Christian E.

Jaszi, George, see comments, page 122.

Jennings, A. R.

Keena, Martin

King, Earle C., see dissent, page 122.

Knauth, Oswald W., see comments, page 135.

Lundvall, A. E., see dissent, page 123.

May, George O., see comments, page 135.

Powlison, Keith

Sanders, T. H.

Saulnier, R. J.

Scovill, Hiram T., see comments, page 124.

Smith, Charles W., see dissent, page 124.

Stephan, Frederick F., see comments, page 128.

Stewart, J. Harold

Warburton, Clark, see comments, page 128.

Werntz, William W., see dissent, page 130.

West, Phillip L.

Wilcox, Edward B., see dissent, page 133.

Yntema, Theodore O.

In addition to the above the following were at one time members of the Study Group or have participated in its work but because of their official position, absence from the country, illness, or for other reasons have not participated in the final report and have neither approved nor disapproved it.

Alexander, Sidney
Blough, Roy
Bronfenbrenner, Martin
Copeland, Morris A.
Cumberland, W. W.
Franke, William B.
Garner, S. Paul
Gilbert, Milton
Hazlitt, Henry

Jackson, J. Hugh
Kuznets, Simon
Nourse, Edwin K.
Reed, Philip D.
Ruggles, Richard
Shishkin, Boris
Slichter, Sumner
Surrey, Stanley S.

MEMBERS OF THE EXECUTIVE COMMITTEE

Bailey, George D.
Barnard, Chester I.
Broad, Samuel J.

Brundage, Percival F.
Dean, Arthur H.
Fabricant, Solomon

EXHIBIT 11

PRICES AND WAGES—1850–1950 (Wholesale Commodity Index; Wages per Hour Correlated to Same Base Year, 1926 = 100)

Prepared by Dun & Bradstreet, Inc.

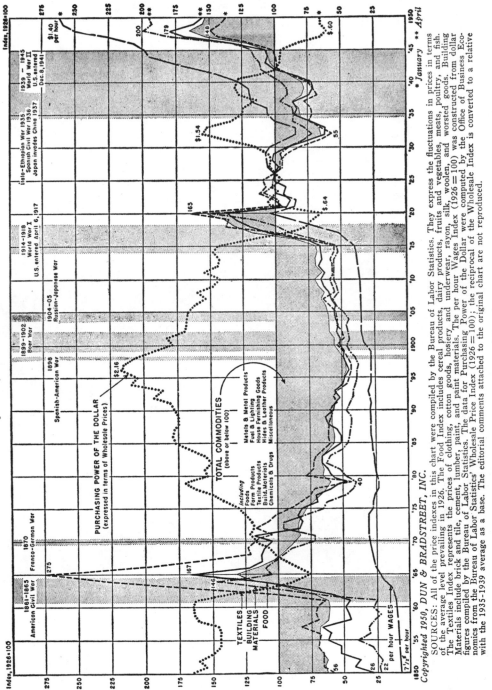

Copyrighted 1950, DUN & BRADSTREET, INC.

SOURCES: All of the price indexes in this chart were compiled by the Bureau of Labor Statistics. They express the fluctuations in prices in terms of the average level prevailing in 1926. The Food Index includes cereal products, dairy products, fruits and vegetables, meats, poultry, and fish. The Textiles Index represents the prices of clothing, cotton goods, hosiery, and underwear, rayon, silk, woolen, and worsted goods. Building Materials include brick and tile, cement, lumber, paint, and paint materials. The per hour Wages Index (1926 = 100) was constructed from dollar figures compiled by the Bureau of Labor Statistics. The data for Purchasing Power of the Dollar were computed by the Office of Business Economics from the Bureau of Labor Statistics' Wholesale Price Index (1926 = 100); the reciprocal of the Wholesale Index is converted to a relative with the 1935–1939 average as a base. The editorial comments attached to the original chart are not reproduced.

145

Bibliography

I. PUBLICATIONS OF THE STUDY GROUP

1. *An Inquiry into the Nature of Business Income Under Present Price Levels,* by Arthur H. Dean (Feb., 1949).
2. *Business Income and Price Levels—An Accounting Study,* by George O. May (July, 1949).
3. *Five Monographs on Business Income* (July, 1950):
   - (*a*) "Income Measurement in a Dynamic Economy," by Sidney S. Alexander.
   - (*b*) "Business Income Concepts in the Light of Monetary Theory," by Martin Bronfenbrenner.
   - (*c*) "Business Costs and Business Income Under Changing Price Levels," by Solomon Fabricant.
   - (*d*) "The Varied Impact of Inflation on the Calculation of Business Income," by Solomon Fabricant.
   - (*e*) "Monetary Theory and the Price Level Trend in the Future," by Clark Warburton.

   Discussion of Monographs. Meeting of Study Group on Business Income, May 13, 1950.

   "The Case Against Change in Present Methods of Accounting for Exhaustion of Business Property," by George O. May (prepared at the request of the Chairman of the Study Group).
4. "The Case Against Price-Level Adjustments in Income Determination," by Howard C. Greer and Edward B. Wilcox, *Illinois Certified Public Accountant,* Vol. 13, No. 1 (Sept., 1950), pp. 1–14; reprinted in *Journal of Accountancy,* Vol. 90, No. 6 (Dec., 1950), pp. 492–504.

II. ARTICLES OR ADDRESSES ON CONCEPTS OF INCOME BY MEMBERS OF THE STUDY GROUP (See also LIFO)

BAILEY, GEORGE D.

"Increasing Significance of the Income Statement," *Journal of Accountancy,* Vol. 85, No. 1 (Jan., 1948), pp. 10–19.

"Problems in Reporting Corporation Income: I, Development of Accounting Principles," *Harvard Business Review,* Vol. 26, No. 5 (Sept., 1948), pp.

513–526; "II, Concepts of Income," *Harvard Business Review,* Vol. 26, No. 6 (Nov., 1948), pp. 680–692 (Dickinson Lectures, 1948, Harvard University, Graduate School of Business Administration).

"Relationship of Accounting to Other Factors in Accurate Reporting of Inflationary Income," *Journal of Accountancy,* Vol. 86, No. 5 (Nov., 1948), pp. 361–369.

"Economic Restrictions on Earnings Determined Under Present Accounting Conventions," *Journal of Accountancy,* Vol. 87, No. 1 (Jan., 1949), pp. 77–80. Excerpts from testimony on Dec. 7, 1948, before the Subcommittee of the Joint Committee on the Economic Report (Flanders Committee).

BARKIN, SOLOMON

"A Trade Unionist Views Net Income Determination," *N.A.C.A. Bulletin,* Vol. 32, No. 10, Sec. 1 (June, 1951), pp. 1193–1206. Challenged in this paper are charges included in income statements, which benefit members of four groups characterized as entrepreneurial.

BLACKIE, WILLIAM

"What is Accounting Accounting for—Now?" (address at Technical Session of the Annual Conference of National Association of Cost Accountants, June, 1948), *N.A.C.A. Bulletin,* Vol. 29, No. 21, Sec. 1 (July 1, 1948), pp. 1349–1378. The nature and measurement of business capital and income in a changing price economy and the use of price indexes for converting original into current money cost.

BROAD, SAMUEL J.

"Effects of Price Level Changes on Financial Statements" (address at Technical Session of the Annual Conference of National Association of Cost Accountants, June, 1948), *N.A.C.A. Bulletin,* Vol. 29, No. 21, Sec. 1 (July 1, 1948), pp. 1329–1348. How "index depreciation" on adjusted original cost might be used to convert depreciation charges into current dollars.

"Business Costs and Business Income Under Changing Price Levels—the Accountant's Point of View," *New Responsibilities of the Accounting Profession,* Papers presented at the Sixty-first Annual Meeting of the American Institute of Accountants, Chicago, 1948, pp. 32–36.

"The Development of Accounting Standards to Meet Changing Economic Conditions," *Journal of Accountancy,* Vol. 87, No. 5 (May, 1949), pp. 378–389. Recent improvement in standards, limitations of the cost basis, and analysis of problems that surround any abandonment of cost.

"Recent Efforts to Increase Significance of the Figure of Net Income," *Journal of Accountancy,* Vol. 89, No. 5 (May, 1950), pp. 376–381 (based on a paper written for the Graduate Study Conference, Rutgers University, Sept., 1949).

BRUNDAGE, PERCIVAL F.
"Three Year Study of Business Income, Its Concepts and Terminology, Started by Institute," *Journal of Accountancy*, Vol. 84, No. 2 (Aug., 1947), pp. 116–117.
"Milestones on the Path of Accounting," *Harvard Business Review*, Vol. 29, No. 4 (July, 1951), pp. 71–81; "Roadblocks in the Path of Accounting," *Harvard Business Review*, Vol. 29, No. 5 (Sept., 1951), pp. 110–119 (Dickinson Lectures, 1951, Harvard University, Graduate School of Business Administration).

CONTROLLERS INSTITUTE OF AMERICA
"What Is Business Income?": The Controller's Viewpoint, by Christian E. Jarchow, pp. 3–17; The Accountant's Viewpoint, by George O. May, pp. 18–30; The Attorney's Viewpoint, by Arthur H. Dean, pp. 31–51. Papers delivered before the Southern Regional Conference of the Controllers Institute of America (March 3–4, 1950), Houston, Texas.

COPELAND, MORRIS A.
"Suitable Accounting Conventions to Determine Business Income," *Journal of Accountancy*, Vol. 87, No. 2 (Feb., 1949), pp. 107–111 (based on a statement prepared by the author for the Study Group on Business Income). Accountants in choosing the conventions should observe the two canons of accounting certainty and economic suitability.

DEAN, ARTHUR H.
"Accounting for the Cost of Pensions—A Lien on Production: I, Legal and Economic Background," *Harvard Business Review*, Vol. 28, No. 4 (July, 1950), pp. 25–40; "II, Possible Ways of Accounting for the Cost of Pensions," *Harvard Business Review*, Vol. 28, No. 5 (Sept., 1950), pp. 102–122 (Dickinson Lectures, 1950, Harvard University, Graduate School of Business Administration).

HASKELL, JOHN
"Illusory Phases of Corporate Profits," *The Exchange*, Vol. 9, No. 4 (April, 1948), pp. 3–4.

JARCHOW, CHRISTIAN E.
"Industry Reports to the Consumer on Prices, Costs and Profits," *The Controller*, Vol. 16, No. 10 (Oct., 1948), pp. 504–508. Paper delivered at the Tenth Annual Institute on Accounting at Ohio State University, Columbus, 1948; *Proceedings* (1948), pp. 65–80.

KING, EARLE C.
"The Income Statement—Problem Child of Accountancy," *New York Certified Public Accountant*, Vol. 18, No. 6 (June, 1948), pp. 413–419. Re-

affirms the S.E.C. support of the "all-inclusive" statement in discussing various Accounting Research Bulletins.

MAY, GEORGE O.

"A Restudy of the Concepts and Terminology of Business Income," *New York Certified Public Accountant,* Vol. 18, No. 1 (Jan., 1948), pp. 9–17.

"Postulates of Income Accounting," *Journal of Accountancy,* Vol. 86, No. 2 (Aug., 1948), pp. 107–111.

"Income, Its Concepts and Terminology," round-table discussion of the Sixty-first Annual Meeting of the American Institute of Accountants, Chicago, Sept., 1948 (unpublished).

"Accounting Research," *Accounting Research* (London), Vol. 1, No. 1 (Nov., 1948), pp. 13–19.

"Profits and High Prices," *The Accountant* (London), Vol. 120, No. 3876 (April 2, 1949), pp. 258–260.

"Study Group on Concepts and Terminology of Business Income," *Accounting and Tax Problems in the Fifties,* Paper presented at the Sixty-second Annual Meeting of the American Institute of Accountants, Los Angeles, 1949, pp. 50–55; "Summary of Report," *Journal of Accountancy,* Vol. 89, No. 1 (Jan., 1950), p. 54.

"Truth and Usefulness in Accounting," *Journal of Accountancy,* Vol. 89, No. 5 (May, 1950), p. 387.

"Business Income," *The Accountant* (London), Vol. 123, No. 3954 (Sept. 30, 1950), pp. 315–323 (based on a series of three lectures delivered during 1950 in Birmingham, Manchester, and London).

SLICHTER, SUMNER

"Are Profits Too High?" *The Atlantic Monthly* (July, 1948), pp. 31–35.

"The Business Outlook," *Commercial and Financial Chronicle,* Vol. 168, No. 4736 (Sept. 23, 1948), pp. 1197, 1220–1221.

"Profits in a Laboristic Society," *Harvard Business Review,* Vol. 27, No. 3 (May, 1949), pp. 346–361.

SMITH, CHARLES W.

"What Concept of Depreciation for Fixed Assets Is Most Useful Today?" *Journal of Accountancy,* Vol. 92, No. 2 (Aug., 1951), pp. 166–174.

WILCOX, EDWARD B.

"A Concept of Business Income," written for the Study Group on Business Income in 1949 (unpublished).

"Accountant's Responsibility for Disclosure of Events After Balance Sheet Date," *Journal of Accountancy,* Vol. 89, No. 4 (April, 1950), pp. 286–297.

III. GENERAL

ALBAN, SIR FREDERICK J.
"The Accounting Vista—Company and National," address at the Chartered Institute of Secretaries Country Conference, Weston-Super-Mare (Sept., 1950), 23 pp.

THE ACCOUNTANT (LONDON)
"The Use of Published Accounts," addresses delivered to members of the London and District Society of Chartered Accountants: I, The Viewpoint of an Investor, by H. Nutcombe Hume, Vol. 123, No. 3965 (Dec. 16, 1950), pp. 610–616; II, The Viewpoint of an Economist, by Roland Bird, Vol. 124, No. 3972 (Feb. 3, 1951), pp. 101–106; III, The Viewpoint of a Creditor, by L. C. Mather, Vol. 124, No. 3981 (April 7, 1951), pp. 330–336; IV, An Accountant's Opinions, by W. H. Lawson, Vol. 124, No. 3983 (April 21, 1951), pp. 383–388.

AMERICAN ACCOUNTING ASSOCIATION
"Price Level Changes and Financial Statements," Supplementary Statement No. 2 by the Committee on Concepts and Standards Underlying Corporate Financial Statements (Aug. 1, 1951).

BAKER, ROBERT O.
"Accounting and the National Economy," *The Controller,* Vol. 16, No. 4 (April, 1948), pp. 184–186. Specific apportionment of economic income depends upon a multitude of economic factors and social concepts over which accounting has no direct control, in spite of being forced to accept increasing responsibility because of them.

BOWLBY, JOEL M.
"Business Costs and Business Income Under Changing Price Levels—Management's Point of View," *New Responsibilities of the Accounting Profession,* Papers presented at the Sixty-first Annual Meeting of the American Institute of Accountants, Chicago, 1948, pp. 23–31.

BRAY, F. SEWELL
"Nature of Income and Capital," *Accounting Research* (London), Vol. 1, No. 1 (Nov., 1948), pp. 27–49. Contrasts English and American usage by comparing definitions of economic and accounting terms.

BRAY, F. SEWELL, AND STONE, RICHARD
"The Presentation of the Central Government Accounts," *Accounting Research* (London), Vol. 1, No. 1 (Nov., 1948), pp. 1–12. Suggested alternative forms of Revenue and Resting (Capital Incomings and Outgoings) Accounts and Balance Sheet for Exchequer, Publicly Controlled Merchanting and Production Enterprises, and National Insurance Funds.

BYRD, KENNETH F.

"The Effect of a Fluctuating Monetary Unit on the Income Statement," *Cost and Management,* Vol. 23, No. 2 (Feb., 1949), pp. 49–60. Ways (including use of price-index figures) to counteract the effect on accounts of the present inflation.

CHAMBERS, STANLEY P.

"Taxation and the Supply of Capital for Industry," *Lloyds Bank Review* (London), New Series, No. 11 (Jan., 1949), pp. 1–20. Urges special fixed allowances in respect of old assets equal to wear-and-tear allowance given for 1945–1946.

COOPER, WILLIAM W.

"Index-Number Adjustments of Financial Statements," *Illinois Certified Public Accountant,* Vol. 13, No. 1 (Sept., 1950), pp. 15–23. An inquiry into the nature of index numbers proposed as a basis for financial reporting.

THE ECONOMIST (LONDON)

"What Are Profits?" Vol. 154, No. 5468 (June 12, 1948), pp. 977–978. A defective economic outlook and accounting technique cloud the realization that an apparent increase in net capital formation is produced by the method of calculating depreciation.

"The Age of Inflation," three articles by a correspondent, Vol. 161, Nos. 5634–5636 (Aug. 18–25, Sept. 1, 1951), and a fourth article expressing the editorial views of *The Economist,* Vol. 161, No. 5637 (Sept. 8, 1951), pp. 542–543 (reprinted as a pamphlet).

EDEY, HAROLD C.

"Measurement of Real Income," *The Accountant* (London), Vol. 120, No. 3867 (Jan. 29, 1949), p. 76. Stewardship principle requires supplementing after further study of the nature and concept of business income, because entrepreneurial decisions in relation to expected future income are required before present income can be ascertained.

FOULKE, ROY A.

A Study of the Theory of Corporate Net Profits (1949), 97 pp. "Net profits after taxes" is a relative mathematical figure; balance sheets should show current economic values of all items, and net-worth and profit-and-loss statements should show dollar-net profits and losses and real-net profits and losses.

FREEMAN, E. STEWART

"Capital Price Adjustment Method for Deflating Inflated Profits," *N.A.C.A. Bulletin,* Vol. 29, No. 11, Sec. 1 (Feb. 1, 1948), pp. 635–658. Proposed third approach to revaluation.

"How to Show Effects of Change in Value of Dollar Yet Preserve Cost

Basis in Accounts," *Journal of Accountancy,* Vol. 85, No. 2 (Feb., 1948), pp. 113–117. Both articles discuss measurement and disclosure of effect of changes in purchasing power of money.

GOODENOUGH, SIR WILLIAM
"Statement on the Report for the Year 1948 of Barclays Bank Limited," reprinted in *The Economist* (London), Vol. 156, No. 5500 (Jan. 22, 1949), pp. 164–166. Shortage of industrial capital.

GRADY, PAUL
"Impact of Economic Income, or Replacement Costs, on Public Utilities," *Replacement Costs and Depreciation Policies* (Controllers Institute of America, 1948), pp. 29–37. Would accept provision for plant exhaustion at current price level similar to LIFO if estimates are objectively determined and the method is consistently followed.

GRAHAM, WILLARD J.
"The Effect of Changing Price Levels Upon the Determination, Reporting and Interpretation of Income," *Accounting Review,* Vol. 24, No. 1 (Jan., 1949), pp. 15–26.

GREAT BRITAIN, COMMITTEE ON THE TAXATION OF TRADING PROFITS
"Report of the Committee" (April, 1951).

HEYWORTH, SIR GEOFFREY
"Essential Maintenance of Capital," remarks in 1948 Annual Report of Lever Brothers & Unilever Ltd., *The Times* (London), Aug. 27, 1948.

JOINT EXPLORATORY COMMITTEE
Some Accounting Terms and Concepts (Cambridge University Press, 1951). Report of the Joint Exploratory Committee appointed by the Institute of Chartered Accountants in England and Wales and by the National Institute of Economic and Social Research.

JONES, RALPH C.
"The Effect of Inflation on Capital and Profits: The Record of Nine Steel Companies," *Journal of Accountancy,* Vol. 87, No. 1 (Jan., 1949), pp. 9–26. Meager common dividends of steel industry in 1940–1947 derived from "real" losses suffered by its creditors and holders of preferred stock.

KENDRICK, H. W.
"The Relationship of Cost Accounting to Income Determination," *Accounting Review,* Vol. 23, No. 1 (Jan., 1948), pp. 35–39.

LELAND, THOMAS W.
"Revenue, Expense and Income," *Accounting Review,* Vol. 23, No. 1 (Jan., 1948), pp. 16–23. Report of the American Accounting Association Committee on Revision of the Statement of Principles.

MANN, A. H., AND KEOWN, K. C.
"The Law Relating to the Divisible Profits and Dividends of Limited Liability Companies," *The Australian Accountant,* Vol. 18, No. 9 (Oct., 1948), pp. 345–362. (Third Commonwealth Institute of Accountants Research Lecture, University of Sydney [Australia], Sept. 9. 1948.)

MASON, PERRY
"A Reconsideration of Criteria of Realization of Business Income" (paper delivered at the Twelfth Annual Institute on Accounting at Ohio State University, Columbus, 1950), *Proceedings* (1950), pp. 89–95.

MILLER, HERMANN C.
"Accounting and Economic Business Profit," *Cost and Management,* Vol. 24, No. 9 (Oct., 1950), pp. 298–312. Discussion of recent writings on concepts of business income and profit, including those of the American Institute of Accountants Study Group, using the economic theories of J. M. Keynes as a basis of comparison.

MOONITZ, MAURICE
"Adaptations to Price-Level Changes," *Accounting Review,* Vol. 23, No. 2 (April, 1948), pp. 137–147. Problem from viewpoint of a permanently higher price level as well as that of a possibly temporary cyclical rise.

MYER, JOHN N.
"Depreciation and Recovery of Cost," *New York Certified Public Accountant,* Vol. 19, No. 5 (May, 1949), pp. 303–304. Depreciation charge currently mistaken by some writers as means of recovery of the investment.

NORRIS, HARRY
"Depreciation Allocations in Relation to Financial Capital, Real Capital and Productive Capacity," *Accounting Research* (London), Vol. 1, No. 2 (July, 1949), pp. 121–132. Financial questions connected with level of real capital used up in earning of revenue.

PARKINSON, BRADBURY B.
"Profits, Accountants and Economists: The Filter Theory and an Equity Solution," *The Accountant* (London), Vol. 124, No. 3984 (April 28, 1951), pp. 402–404. Abstract of an address to the Liverpool Economic and Statistical Society, Jan. 26, 1951.

PATON, WILLIAM A.
"Accounting Procedures and Private Enterprise," *Journal of Accountancy,* Vol. 85, No. 4 (April, 1948), pp. 278–291. A plea for realistic recording, and a discussion of the effect on income of misstatement of assets.

PELOUBET, MAURICE E.
"Are We Giving Away Our Capital Without Knowing It?" *New York Certified Public Accountant,* Vol. 18, No. 6 (June, 1948), pp. 440–445. Need

for objective analysis and appraisal of elements involved in the problem of replacement depreciation.

PREST, A. R.
"Replacement Cost Depreciation," *Accounting Research* (London), Vol. 1, No. 4 (July, 1950), pp. 385–402.

ROSS, CLARENCE H.
"Compensating for Dollar Inflation in Rate Regulation," *Public Utilities Fortnightly,* Vol. 47, No. 11 (May 24, 1951), pp. 663–673. A proposed solution to problems created in rate making by the continued inflation of the dollar.

SANDERS, THOMAS H.
"Income and Surplus," *New York Certified Public Accountant,* Vol. 18, No. 9 (Sept., 1948), pp. 647–651. A discussion of what constitutes "actual net income."
"The Annual Report: Portrait of a Business," *Harvard Business Review,* Vol. 27, No. 1 (Jan., 1949), pp. 1–12.
"Depreciation and 1949 Price Levels," *Harvard Business Review,* Vol. 27, No. 3 (May, 1949), pp. 293–307; "Two Concepts of Accounting," *Harvard Business Review,* Vol. 27, No. 4 (July, 1949), pp. 505–520 (Dickinson Lectures, 1949, Harvard University, Graduate School of Business Administration).

SMITH, DAN THROOP
"Business Profits During Inflation," *Harvard Business Review,* Vol. 26, No. 2 (March, 1948), pp. 216–229.

SMITH, DAN THROOP, AND BUTTERS, J. KEITH
Taxable and Business Income (National Bureau of Economic Research, Inc., 1949), 342 pp.

THE TIMES (LONDON)
"Profits and Prices," editorial, June 4, 1949. Criticizes attack by Chancellor of the Exchequer on the level of profits (during debate on the Finance Bill) as "confusing the issue."

U.S. CONGRESS, JOINT COMMITTEE ON THE ECONOMIC REPORT,
     SUBCOMMITTEE ON PROFITS
Corporate Profits. Hearings, 80th Congress, 2nd sess., Dec. 6–21, 1948 (1949).

U.S. DEPARTMENT OF COMMERCE, NATIONAL INCOME DIVISION
National Income and Product of the United States 1929–46—1929–50 (1947, 1951), 2 vols. See particularly 1951 ed., Parts II and III, and Statistical Tables 1 and 22.

WALLACE, EDWARD L.
"A Rationale of Income Determination, the Current Cost of Productive Equivalents Concept," *N.A.C.A. Bulletin,* Vol. 30, No. 18, Sec. 1 (May 15, 1949), pp. 1027–1038.

WELCKER, JOHN W.
"Divergent Views on Corporate Profits," *Harvard Business Review,* Vol. 17, No. 2 (March, 1949), pp. 250–264. Discusses four conflicting statements regarding industry's profit position: testimony by Sumner Slichter and Stanley Ruttenberg (Congress of Industrial Organizations) at congressional hearings; an article in *The National City Bank of New York Monthly Letter on Economic Conditions, Government Finance* (Nov., 1948), p. 127; and an item in *Survey of Current Business* (Dec., 1948), p. 7.

WELLINGTON, C. OLIVER
"Accounting Income vs. Economic Income," *Canadian Chartered Accountant,* Vol. 54, No. 1 (Jan., 1949), pp. 27–34.

WIXON, RUFUS
"The Measurement and Administration of Income," *Accounting Review,* Vol. 24, No. 2 (April, 1949), pp. 184–190.

WYMAN, GEORGE F.
"Is Surplus *the* Reserve?" *Accounting Review,* Vol. 23, No. 3 (July, 1948), pp. 285–288. Surplus is perhaps the only reserve appropriate to corporate accounting, in which case the word would no longer trouble accountants or mislead lay readers.

IV. LIFO

AMERICAN INSTITUTE OF ACCOUNTANTS, RESEARCH DEPARTMENT
"Use of LIFO by Industry Groups," *Journal of Accountancy,* Vol. 86, No. 1 (July, 1948), pp. 68–69. Tabular analysis of seventy-five companies.
"Should Estimated Current Value of Inventories Be Disclosed?" *Journal of Accountancy,* Vol. 88, No. 3 (Sept., 1949), pp. 218–221.

BELL, HERMON F.
"Last-in, First-out, or LIFO Method of Inventory Determination with Especial Reference to Retailers," *New York Certified Public Accountant,* Vol. 19, No. 9 (Sept., 1949), pp. 537–541, 548.

BLACKETT, GEORGE H., AND LADIN, DAVID
"Disadvantages of LIFO for a Growing Retail Establishment," *Journal of Accountancy,* Vol. 88, No. 1 (July, 1949), pp. 58–62. Table of computations for twenty-five years reinforces statement that future tax liability is greater under LIFO.

BLISS, CHARLES A.

"The Reality of Inventory Profits," *Harvard Business Review,* Vol. 26, No. 5 (Sept., 1948), pp. 527–542. Includes impact of LIFO method on profits.

BLOUGH, CARMAN G.

"Inventory Reserves," *Illinois Certified Public Accountant,* Vol. 10, No. 3 (March, 1948), pp. 67–72. Address at Accounting Conference sponsored by Illinois Society of Certified Public Accountants.

"Reserves for Involuntarily Liquidated Inventories Under the LIFO Method," *Journal of Accountancy,* Vol. 85, No. 3 (March, 1948), pp. 204–206. Comparison to provision in current expenses for replacement of fixed assets.

"Changing Accounting and Economic Concepts Affect Methods of Inventory Pricing," *Journal of Accountancy,* Vol. 86, No. 3 (Sept., 1948), pp. 204–212. Measuring inventory costs, allocating them to accounting periods, the use of LIFO and reserves for future price declines.

BUTTERS, J. KEITH, ASSISTED BY POWELL NILAND

Effects of Taxation—Inventory Accounting and Policies (Harvard University, Graduate School of Business Administration, Division of Research, 1949), xix + 330 pp. Largely a discussion of LIFO.

COPES, RAYMOND F.

"The Case for Adopting LIFO Now," *Stores,* Vol. 32, No. 9 (Sept., 1950), pp. 36–37, table.

FREUDENTHAL, DAVID M., AND OEHLER, ARNOLD J.

"Should LIFO Be Adopted?" *The Balance Sheet,* Vol. 19, No. 5 (Jan., 1951), pp. 11–17, chart, tables. Freudenthal argues for adoption, Oehler against it.

FRIEDMAN, J. P.

"Bureau Permits Use of LIFO by Retailers for Tax Purposes," *Journal of Accountancy,* Vol. 85, No. 2 (Feb., 1948), pp. 118–125. Explains changes in calculations for LIFO requiring amended returns.

"Should Retailers Adopt LIFO This Year?" *New York Certified Public Accountant,* Vol. 20, No. 12 (Dec., 1950), pp. 716–720.

JARCHOW, CHRISTIAN E.

"How Do We Stand with Inflation? A Defense of Conventional Accounting," *N.A.C.A. Bulletin,* Vol. 31, No. 6, Sec. 1 (Feb., 1950), pp. 687–698. Review of discussion on LIFO and depreciation.

LITTLETON, A. C.

"Inventory Disclosures," *New York Certified Public Accountant,* Vol. 18, No. 11 (Nov., 1948), pp. 807–810.

McAnly, H. T.
"Curbing the Effect of Our Erratic Dollar in Pricing Inventories and Providing for Depreciation," *New York Certified Public Accountant,* Vol. 18, No. 8 (Aug., 1948), pp. 573–582.

"Recognizing Current Price Levels in the Profit and Loss Statement and in the Balance Sheet" (paper presented at the Twelfth Annual Institute on Accounting at Ohio State University, Columbus, 1950), *Proceedings* (1950), pp. 72–88.

"LIFO Now for All Inventory Pricing," *New York Certified Public Accountant,* Vol. 21, No. 7 (July, 1951), pp. 483–492.

"The Need for Agreement on a Uniform Basis of Inventory Valuation; LIFO with Simple Equitable Tax-Law Revision Provides the Solution," *The Controller,* Vol. 19, No. 8 (Aug., 1951), pp. 347–351, 382–383.

McAnly, H. T., and Blackie, William
"Current Trends in the Evaluation of Assets," *Illinois Certified Public Accountant,* Vol. 11, No. 3 (March, 1949), pp. 16–27. Paper presented at a Business Problems School sponsored jointly by the Chicago Association of Commerce and Industry and the Illinois Society of Certified Public Accountants, Nov. 9, 1948.

Miller, Charles R.
"The LIFO Method of Inventory Pricing," *Illinois Certified Public Accountant,* Vol. 11, No. 3 (March, 1949), pp. 10–15.

Moonitz, Maurice
"Adaptations to Price-Level Changes," *Accounting Review,* Vol. 23, No. 2 (April, 1948), pp. 137–147.

Nad, Leon M.
"How to Simplify Use of LIFO by the Dollar-value Method of Calculating Inventories," *Journal of Accountancy,* Vol. 91, No. 2 (Feb., 1951), pp. 226–271.

National Retail Dry Goods Association, Controllers' Congress
"LIFO: A Review" (1951), 15 pp., tables.

Peloubet, Maurice E.
"Has LIFO Fallen?" *Journal of Accountancy,* Vol. 85, No. 4 (April, 1948), pp. 298–303. Confutes Wilcox arguments (*infra*) on comparability of statements, Treasury attitudes, etc.

"Disclosure of Current Value of LIFO Inventories Is Not Normally Useful; the Figure Must Be an Estimate Based on an Unreal Situation," *Journal of Accountancy,* Vol. 89, No. 6 (June, 1950), pp. 487–489.

Stewart, J. Harold
"Letter Favoring Disclosure of Replacement Value of LIFO Inventories," *Journal of Accountancy,* Vol. 86, No. 2 (Aug., 1948), pp. 158–159.

U.S. BUREAU OF LABOR STATISTICS

"Department Store Inventory Price Indexes for Each January and July 1941–1951" (1948–1951). Prepared in cooperation with the Bureau of Internal Revenue and the American Retail Federation; to be used by department stores employing the LIFO method of accounting.

U.S. HOUSE OF REPRESENTATIVES

"A Bill Relating to the Use for Federal Tax Purposes of the Last-in, First-out Inventory Method," 82nd Congress, 1st sess. H.R. 934 (Jan. 4, 1951).

WALTER, JAMES E.

"Last-in, First-out," *Accounting Review,* Vol. 25, No. 1 (Jan., 1950), pp. 63–75.

WELLINGTON, C. OLIVER

"LIFO Fails Only When It Is Improperly Applied" (a letter), *Journal of Accountancy,* Vol. 85, No. 3 (March, 1948), p. 231.

WILCOX, EDWARD B.

"The Rise and Fall of LIFO," *Journal of Accountancy,* Vol. 85, No. 2 (Feb., 1948), pp. 98–103. LIFO should be curtailed because its use results in uncertainty.

WILES, PETER

"Corporation Taxation Based on Replacement Cost," *Accounting Research* (London), Vol. 2, No. 1 (Jan., 1951), pp. 77–82.

V. CORPORATE REPORTS

UNITED STATES

American Institute of Accountants, Research Department: *Accounting Trends in Corporate Reports, Twelve Months Ending June 30, 1948; Accounting Techniques Used in Published Corporate Annual Reports, Fiscal Years Ending July 1, 1948, to June 30, 1949; Accounting Trends and Techniques in Published Corporate Annual Reports, Fiscal Years Ending July 1, 1949, to June 30, 1950.* Annual cumulative surveys of the accounting aspects of 525 corporate annual reports, to which are added excerpts from, and comments upon, unusual accounting treatments found in many additional reports.

GREAT BRITAIN

IMPERIAL CHEMICAL INDUSTRIES LTD.

In the accounts of this company as at December 31, 1950, fixed assets have been restated on the basis of January 1, 1950 costs, and depreciation provisions have been made on the increased costs.

LEVER BROTHERS & UNILEVER LTD.—Annual Report for the Year 1950

Unilever has made important dispositions against the risk of falling prices. The change to a LIFO basis for the American subsidiary and the strengthening of the reserves against stock are clear examples.

The group has also continued the practice of fortifying the current year's depreciation provision with a large appropriation against the replacement of fixed assets, thereby meeting the full burden of replacement on assets "used up" during the year, though the depreciation provisions for the entire period before this practice was adopted would still be insufficient to provide for replacement at current price levels.—*The Economist* (London), Vol. 160, No. 5626 (June 23, 1951), p. 1519.